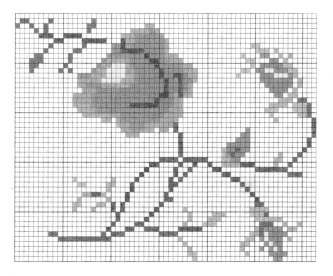

cross stitch

cross stitch

projects · techniques · motifs

Gloria Nicol

Photography by Debbie Patterson

Quadrille

page 1: Rose Tablecloth (see page 40)
page 2: Shelf Edging (see page 82)
page 3: Gingham Tablemats (see page 48)
page 5: Strawberry Ribbon Throw (see page 62)

Detail photography · Dave King
Illustrations · Keith Jackson, Colin Salmon

First published in 1995 by
Quadrille Publishing Limited
9 Irving Street, London WC2H 7AT

Published in association with the National Magazine Company Limited
Country Living is a trademark of the National Magazine Company Limited

Copyright © Text, design and layout 1995 Quadrille Publishing Limited
Copyright © Project photography 1995 Debbie Patterson
Copyright © 1995 Detail photography Dave King

The right of Gloria Nicol to be identified as the author of this work has been asserted by her in
accordance with the Copyright, Designs and Patents Act 1988.

Publishing Director · Anne Furniss
Art Director · Mary Evans
Managing Editor · Jane O'Shea
Editor · Jenny Watson
Copy Editor · Sarah Widdicombe, Jo Weeks
Art Editor · Sue Storey
Production Assistant · Kate Walford

British Library Cataloguing-in-Publication Data
A catalogue record for this book is available
from the British Library.

ISBN 1 899988 25 4

Printed in Hong Kong
Produced by Mandarin Offset Ltd

contents

Introduction

Cross stitch must surely be the most versatile of embroidery stitches. This simple stitch can be used entirely alone to make decorative borders, motifs and panels to embellish plain fabrics. There is something particularly satisfying about working the stitch. The two actions which form each stitch create a perfect and pleasing symmetry which can be repeated to build up dense shapes or to form fine curved and twining lines or delicate openwork patterns.

The first crudely worked cross stitches were used to join animal skins together to provide basic clothing and shelter. From these humble beginnings the stitcher's craft developed and over many centuries evolved from a purely practical method of constructing garments to the highly decorative and ornamental process we know today. The perishability of natural fibres has meant that few examples of early stitching have survived but cloth fragments found at archaeological sites in Egypt dating from about 500AD show the use of cross stitch to decorate the fabric.

Through the ages cross stitch has become an important part of the folk art and craft heritage of countries all around the world. Distinctive pattern and colour variations have developed which are particular to specific countries. In China, cross stitch was almost always worked in dark blue thread on white gauze-like clothing fabric. The European style of embroidery became established during the sixteenth century with brightly dyed threads in red and blue as the predominant colours, often with the addition of brown and black to give outline definition and striking results. Many of these regional variations overlap to create designs that have a universal appeal.

With only one stitch to master and the minimum of materials required, it doesn't take long to become a proficient stitcher. Levels of ability really depend on how much patience the stitcher is blessed with. In essence cross stitch is not at all complicated, but does require staying power to complete the more densely stitched pieces. Over the pages that follow you will find a selection of contemporary and traditional designs that appeal to all different levels of skill.

Beginning cross stitch

Counted cross stitch was one of the traditional peasant embroideries of Europe which was successfully used to decorate many different types of articles, from household linens to everyday clothing. Cross stitches are formed on the right side of the fabric in two parts, a diagonal foundation stitch on the bottom and a diagonal cover stitch on the top; this makes it an easy stitch to learn, as well as to work. Always remember to work each cover stitch slanting in the same direction for a smooth and uniform appearance, being careful not to pierce the threads of fabric as you stitch. Practice will help you to achieve beautifully formed crosses which can then be worked into the charming designs which you will find in this book.

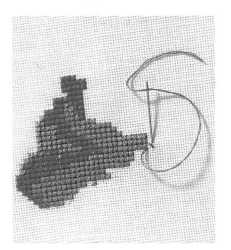

materials

A fine selection of equipment and materials is available for working cross stitch designs. When choosing a fabric, consider whether the finished product needs to be strong and hard-wearing, fine and delicate, plain or patterned. Look for fabrics in your local store, choose from the new ranges of scissors, needles, hoops and frames, and take advantage of the wide choice of embroidery threads which come in a glorious palette of colours.

Fabrics

Fabrics that make a suitable background for cross stitch are of an evenweave type. That is, the number of threads running vertically (warp) exactly matches the number of threads running horizontally (weft), and the resulting mesh provides an even grid of regularly spaced holes for the needle to pass through. The number of fabric threads, or 'blocks' of threads, over a square of 2.5cm (1in) is called the 'count' of the fabric and is a vital consideration when embarking on any cross stitch project. The finer the fabric, the higher the thread count; the coarser the fabric, the lower the thread count (see Stitches and thread counts, opposite).

A fine fabric with a high thread count will produce smaller stitches and therefore provide the opportunity for more intricate patterning than a coarser weave. A coarser fabric, with a low count, will produce larger stitches.

Linen and cotton are the most usual fabrics used for cross stitch, with special evenweave fabrics produced specifically for counted thread work. These can be very expensive, but, fabrics for cross stitch are available in craft outlets, in smaller cut pieces, so look for the size you need, rather than buying full widths of fabric by the metre (yard).

Linen

For centuries, linen, woven with long continuous threads, has been the fabric chosen for making household linens and it is still favoured for its strength and hard-wearing qualities. Although expensive to buy, it is well worth the investment and when embellished with cross stitches can produce exquisite results with the enduring quality of an heirloom. It is available in a wide range of thread counts from coarse and heavy to extremely fine.

Cotton

Hardanger is a cotton fabric woven with warp and weft threads which are arranged evenly in pairs. This gives a more accentuated mesh on which to work and the holes are far easier to see. **Aida** is similar to Hardanger but the warp and weft threads are woven in denser groups, producing an even and accentuated weave that is particularly easy to stitch. Aida is ideal for the beginner. **Check** fabric, where the inherent pattern makes a regular grid to follow in the same way as the holes on an evenweave fabric, is also a suitable background on which to work cross stitch.

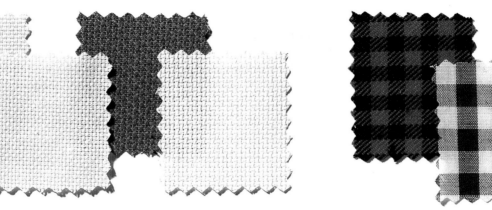

Fabrics with uneven weave

It is possible to work cross stitch patterns on to other fabrics with closer uneven weaves, such as chambray or cotton sheeting, by using waste canvas or a piece of evenweave fabric as a guide.

Waste canvas is available in four different thread counts, from 8 to 16, and is worked with a pointed crewel needle. This is an ideal way to add cross stitch to any fabric, it works better for motifs but it can also be used for borders. It is particularly good for working monograms, which can be placed at an angle and do not need to follow the grain of the fabric (see Using waste canvas, on page 17).

Stitches and thread counts

The thread count determines the finished size of the pattern when it is translated from the chart to the fabric; it also indicates the weight and number of strands of thread needed (see Threads, below). For linens and other fabrics with high counts of between 25 and 55 threads per 2.5cm (1in), the stitches are often worked over two or three threads at a time. This means that if the stitches are worked over two threads at a time on a 28 count fabric, a design with 14 stitches to 2.5cm (1 in) will result.

Threads

For cross stitch, embroidery threads made from cotton, wool and silk are most commonly used. Most of the projects in this book are worked using stranded cotton, which is available in a vast range of lustrous colours. The thread is sold in small skeins made up of six fine strands loosely twisted together. Before use, the thread is separated into single strands and re-formed with one or more strands to the thickness required. The threads can be pulled directly from the skein as you work, or they can be cut into lengths and arranged on card with eyelet holes to hold them neatly in place. Cut maximum lengths of thread between 45cm (18in) and 60cm (24in), as longer threads are likely to become knotted. When working with soft embroidery or pearl cotton, use the thread, as it is, straight from the skein.

Number of strands

The fabric thread count dictates the number of strands of thread used (details are given for each project). Use the following guide when designing your own projects.

number of stitches to 2.5cm (1in)	number of strands of thread	needle size (tapestry)
9	3	24
11	2 or 3	24
14	2	24 or 26
18	1 or 2	26
22	1	26

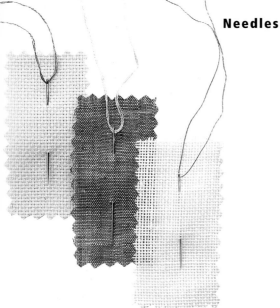

Needles

Blunt-ended tapestry needles are used to make stitches on evenweave fabric, as these push the fabric fibres apart without splitting them. The needle should relate to the size of the holes in the mesh – it should slip easily through the fabric without forcing the threads out of shape, but should be large enough to be held in place by the mesh and not fall through when pushed into the spaces between the threads. The thread count chart shown on page 11 recommends needle sizes for the weight of fabric and the thread that you will be using.

Counted cross stitch is always worked with a tapestry needle except when the fabric requires a pointed needle to be used. Crewel needles are needed on waste canvas to pierce the closely woven fabric underneath. They are also used for working woven check or textured fabric, such as the linen huckaback towel on pages 86–87. Crewel needles come in sizes numbered from 1 to 10. The following chart shows the right size of needle to use with each different weight of fabric.

fabric	number of strands of thread	needle size (crewel)
fine lawn	1 or 2	8
medium lawn, sailcloth	3	7
heavier fabric	4 or pearl cotton	6

Scissors

A pair of good embroidery scissors is a worthwhile investment and an essential tool for cross stitch work. They can also be extremely decorative; antique scissors are a highly collectable and coveted tool of the craft.

The scissors should be small and the blades must end in sharp points that can cut the threads close to the fabric, efficiently and cleanly. On the odd occasions when it is necessary to unpick mistakes, these sharp points really come into their own. It is a good idea to tie a piece of coloured ribbon on to the scissors, so that they are easy to distinguish among coloured embroidery threads and to find if they slip from your lap while you are stitching. Keep them especially for the purpose for which they are intended; do *not* be tempted to cut paper with them or the blades will quickly become spoiled.

Frames

Unlike canvas work, where the stitches completely hide the canvas, cross stitch only covers specific areas and the background fabric is meant to show in some places. This means that the stitches are less likely to distort the fabric, making the use of a frame unnecessary. Whether you decide to use one or not is therefore a matter of personal preference. With a frame the needle is used at a different angle, so it may be a matter of practising to find which method suits you best.

Small, round hand frames, used in pairs, can squash and distort those stitches that are pressed between the two wooden hoops. If you like to work with a frame of this type, it is worth completely covering the hoops with seam binding; you will find that this gives the fabric stretched between the frame something more to adhere to and it also allows the hoops to be fastened less tightly. It is wise to remember to remove the frame before putting away the work each time, otherwise the fabric will lose its shape and become difficult to work with later.

Working conditions

Work in daylight whenever possible and in good, soft, artificial light at other times. Daylight simulation bulbs are inexpensive to buy and are available from artist supply shops and good hardware stores. You will find these kinder to the eyes than common household bulbs and you will notice that colours, particularly threads of similar tones, are easier to distinguish under this light. Attractive workbaskets are widely available in which to store your equipment safely when not in use.

working the stitches

Cross stitch is an easy stitch to work and with only the minimum of practice the basic technique can be mastered quickly. If you are a complete beginner, it is well worth taking some time to learn how to make the stitches correctly and thus form good stitching habits right from the start, which will result in neat, even work. Two simple movements are needed to form each stitch, which soon become second nature, and as stitching becomes quicker and easier it is encouraging to see beautiful patterns developing on the fabric.

Cross stitch

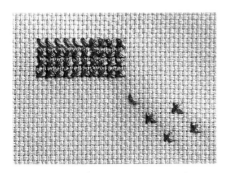

Generally, cross stitches to form blocks of a single colour are worked in rows. A row of half stitches is made in one direction across the fabric and is then completed by crossing back over the stitches in the opposite direction. Most cross stitch designs can be worked in this way, so areas of pattern are filled in quite quickly. Another way is to complete each single stitch, one at a time. Complex and multi-coloured designs, requiring odd stitches in single colours, need to be worked in this way.

Whether the stitches are worked in rows or singly, it is important that the slant of the cover stitch runs in the same direction throughout, except when working patterns made up of blocks of quartered motifs; such as the square bed cushions on page 26, where each part of the block points towards the centre. These can be worked by completing one segment of the motif, then rotating the fabric through a quarter turn to work the next segment, and so on, so that the stitches are all arranged around the centre.

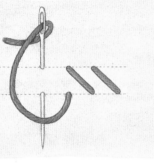

fig 1   fig 2   fig 3   fig 4

Working crosses in rows:
1 Work from right to left, laying down half the crosses in a row (fig1).
2 Work from left to right, inserting the needle at 1 and coming up at 2 (fig 2).

Starting a thread
If you are working a block of stitches, hold the end of a short length of thread at the back so that the stitches you are

Finishing off a thread
At the end of a colour block, or when the thread is getting too short, pull it through to the back and slip the needle under a few stitches of the same colour to hold it firmly in place, then clip the thread close to the fabric to keep the back tidy. When

Working crosses singly:
1 Bring the needle up at 1, insert at 2, and come up at 3, under 2 (fig 3).
2 Bring the needle up at 3 and insert at 4 to cover the foundation stitch (fig 4).

making will catch over it. When working only a few stitches in one colour, catch the thread underneath a few stitches of another colour on the back.

blocks stitched in the same colour are only a short distance apart, catch the thread behind other stitches across the back of the work for continuous stitching. When using finely woven fabrics dark threads can show through on the front, so keep these bridging threads short.

The reverse side

Great emphasis is often placed on the neatness of the back of the work and there are certainly aesthetic advantages in this, especially when it may sometimes be visible, such as on a towel border or along a sheet turnback. In these cases the back of the work should be made up of small straight stitches arranged in neat parallel lines. The back of the stitches on cushions, pillows and samplers is not so crucial, as they will be hidden from view. Do not sacrifice enthusiasm and spontaneity by worrying about such refinements, but again, a little time spent developing a good, even technique is likely to pay off by producing neat stitches on both sides – as a general rule, the condition of the underside is a reflection of the quality of the front.

Unpicking

If you make a mistake, only unpick the stitches if you really have to: when hidden within a patterned panel or densely worked area, a block of stitches sloping in the wrong direction may not be noticeable to anyone but you. If stitches must be unpicked, take care that the fabric threads are not pulled out of line and the holes in the mesh do not become enlarged. Use pointed scissors to cut the thread frequently, so that the strands pulled out are kept short and are therefore easy to remove.

Backstitch

Backstitch can be used to outline a pattern and to add definition to a design, as well as in its own right. This versatile stitch can be worked in all directions to make horizontal and vertical lines as well as diagonals. It helps to break up areas of stitching that might otherwise look too dense and can be used without becoming overpowering. Older sampler designs, often have letters of the alphabet outlined in backstitch.

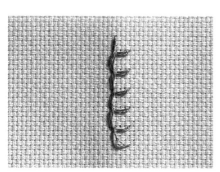

Working the stitch

Using one strand of thread. bring the needle and thread from the back up through the fabric in the first hole. Push it back down into the fabric two threads along, at the same time pointing it forward so that it pushes up through the fabric two threads or more in front of the new stitch. Take a small stitch backwards into the last stitch worked, over as many threads as required; this will generally match the depth of the cross stitches.

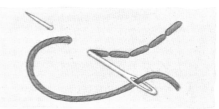

Blanket stitch

Using blanket stitch to finish off a hem is a simple way to add an extra decorative touch to your needlework. As well as edging blankets, such as the child's version on page 36, the stitch can be used in contrasting or complementary colours to embellish the borders of Oxford pillowcases (page 34) and tablecloth hems (pages 40 and 44).

Work from left to right, and keep the stitches to the same depth throughout to make a straight and even border.

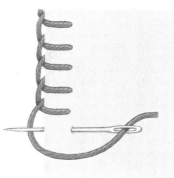

Working the stitch

1 Join the thread to the outside edge and bring the needle over and down into the fabric above this point and slightly to the right of it.
2 Point the needle down the back of the fabric towards the edge and pull it evenly through the loop made by the thread. Repeat, keeping the stitches evenly spaced as you work.

starting

A little time and thought spent in preparation before starting will save you trouble later on. Keep the work crease free and clean and always be generous when cutting out, allowing extra fabric all the way round because a larger piece will be easier to work with. Carefully centre the motif or position the border to ensure a successful finish to your work.

Preparation

Inspect the fabric to be used and iron out any creases before beginning to sew. Avoid fabric that has been folded for some time, as the outside edges of long-standing creases often become stained. If the fabric is soiled, cut it to size avoiding the marks or, if this is impossible, launder it before you begin.

Try to keep the fabric clean while you work – it will save a lot of trouble later on. Wash your hands frequently as you stitch so that the natural oils in your skin do not soil the work, and store it in a workbasket between stitching sessions to help keep it fresh and clean. The fabric will inevitably become crumpled, but can quickly be restored to its original condition by ironing when stitching is complete.

Cutting out

Always cut a piece of fabric larger than is needed for the finished piece; it can be cut down to the correct size when the work is finished. With evenweave fabrics the piece can be cut lengthways or widthways without any appreciable difference in quality, so use whichever way will be most economical. If the project is likely to take some time to complete, it is worth turning under or oversewing the edges on a sewing machine to prevent them becoming frayed. In every project in this book extra fabric has been allowed for trimming to size later.

Positioning the design

The pattern stitches will be applied by working from the middle of the fabric out towards the edges and the design therefore needs to be placed centrally. In order to do this, you will need to mark out the centre of the fabric with lines of tacking stitches.

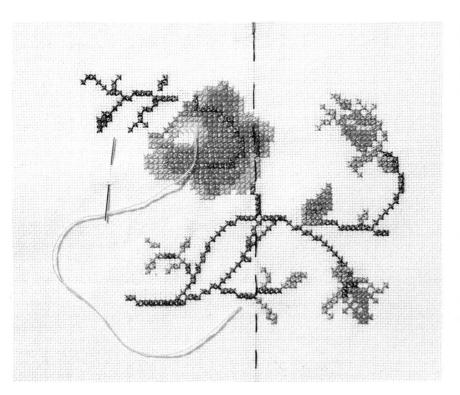

1 Start by folding the piece of fabric in half lengthways and mark the line made by the fold with a pin. Work a row of tacking stitches along the fold line, following the grain of the fabric made by a warp thread.

2 Next, fold the fabric in half widthways and, in the same way as in step 1, mark along the resulting fold with tacking stitches. This time you will be following the line of the weft thread.

Occasionally, it will be necessary to plot a border pattern running around the edges of the design, before you position the central motif or pattern.

If it is necessary to count fabric threads over a large area, you will find it helpful to place pins at 10-thread intervals; you will be surprised how much quicker and easier it is to keep count in this way. However, if you use this method, take care that the weave of the threads does not become distorted by the pins.

Plotting the design

The central point and guidelines are now clearly visible for you to begin plotting the design, following the chart that you have chosen.

Where a motif appears in isolation, it may be easier to mark out its position using tacking thread or a special marking pen, sold for embroidery purposes, which will lightly mark the fabric but disappears in the first wash.

Following a chart

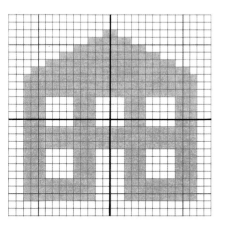

It is important to understand that each square on a chart represents one cross stitch on the fabric. No matter how many fabric threads a cross stitch is worked over, it is always represented by only one square on the chart. The colour of each square corresponds to the colour key listed beside each chart, with thread numbers to indicate the exact colours to use in each case. The thread colours listed for each project are given in the two most widely available brands, Anchor and DMC.

Using waste canvas

1 Cut a piece of waste canvas 5–7cm (2–3in) bigger all round than the design you wish to stitch.

2 Place the canvas on to your fabric where the design is required. Follow the grain of the fabric if the position is meant to be square. To prevent the canvas slipping as well as to mark the central threads for placement of the design, tack it securely in place, with lines of stitching making a cross at the centre as well as around the edges of the canvas. For larger designs, extra lines of tacking may be necessary to secure the canvas in place.

3 Beginning at the centre in the usual way, work the design by stitching into the holes of the canvas and through the fabric beneath, taking care that the needle goes cleanly into the holes and does not pierce the threads of the canvas (pierced threads can be difficult to remove later). Use the number of strands of thread to correspond to the appropriate thread count as normal.

4 When the stitching is complete, remove all the tacking stitches and trim the waste canvas to within 2.5cm (1in) of the stitched area on all sides. Dampen the waste fabric threads until they become limp and then pull them out of the canvas, thread by thread. You may need to use tweezers to do this. Be sure to draw them out low to the fabric and only in the direction in which the canvas threads lie. To remove long threads of waste canvas when working larger designs, it may be helpful to cut the canvas threads between areas of stitching.

Evenweave fabric can be used in the same way as waste canvas and does not require dampening before removing the threads. Take particular care that the threads are not pierced by the needle when stitching if using evenweave fabric as your guide.

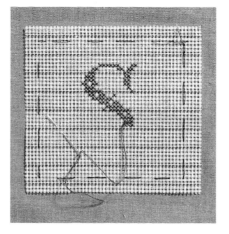

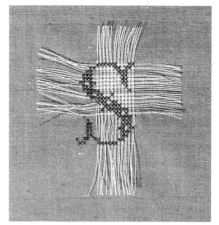

finishing off

When a completed piece has been carefully and painstakingly worked, it is well worth taking the time to make the finishing touches extra special to show off your talent to best advantage. Adding drawn thread work hems to tablecloths and bedlinen gives them a distinctive quality with a traditional character. Mitred corners create an elegant, smooth finish to the right side of the work and have the advantage of looking so much more professional than hems that are simply turned in straight.

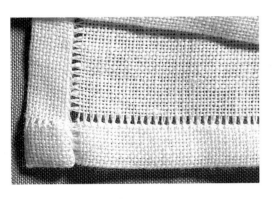

Drawn thread work hem

1 Work out the position of the hem edge and hemline and mark with pins.

2 Pull two of the threads out of the fabric following the hemline, to leave an open band of adjacent threads.

3 Turn up the hem to meet the edge of the drawn threads. Next, pin and tack in place (fig 1).

4 Using a length of sewing thread and a sharp needle, and with the wrong side of the work facing you, bring the needle up through the threads and work the stitches in sequence, catching the hem in place (fig 2). Continue in this way, at the same time pulling the threads of the open band together so as to form a regular and decorative formation.

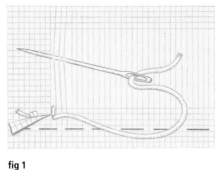

fig 1

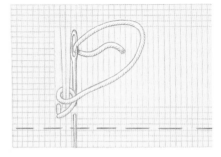

fig 2

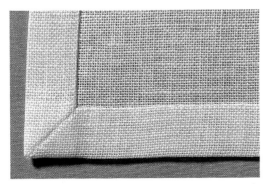

Mitring a corner

1 Along each raw edge, turn a hem of an equal depth of fabric and press to mark the folds (fig 3).

2 Turn over a slightly larger hem to conceal any raw edges completely and press again in the same way.

3 Pin then tack the hem in place to within 10cm (4in) of each corner.

4 Unfold the hem at each corner, revealing the pressed fold lines. Turn in the corner of the fabric to make a right-angled triangle, with the inside corner point exactly touching the centre of the slope of the triangle (fig 4). Press, unfold and trim close to the diagonal fold.

5 Turn this diagonal fold back into the fabric, then fold the hems back in position to make a flat, mitred corner with sloping edges that meet diagonally along the corner (fig 5). Tack and slipstitch all along the hem edge.

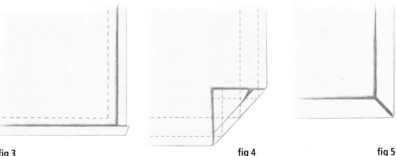

fig 3

fig 4

fig 5

Caring for your work

When the stitching is completed, hopefully the finished piece will be clean, in which case it will simply need a quick pressing with an iron to revitalize it. When a piece has taken a long time to work, however, it may need to be washed and pressed before it is used or framed.

In the past it was generally recommended that hand-hot water and soap-based powder without bleach be used, and that the fabric was washed gently without rubbing, rinsed well and dried flat on a towel. Nowadays, the main manufacturers of embroidery threads tend to advise rather more robust treatment, as the threads are dyed to be colourfast and they launder best in a washing machine with as high a temperature as the fabric will stand, up to 95°C. This certainly has advantages for everyday household linens, which will require many washes throughout their life.

When ironing cross stitch, the iron should never be applied to the right side of the work as this will flatten and spoil the stitches. Instead, make several layers of towelling on the ironing board, place the cross stitched piece face down on them and cover with another piece of fabric. Use the iron at the linen setting and press the work while it is just damp. This way, the stitches will retain their slightly embossed look.

Keep the finished piece out of direct sunlight whenever possible to help prevent the threads losing their vibrancy.

Ageing the fabric

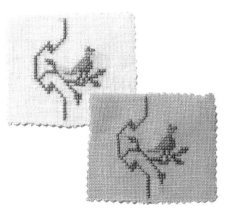

Antique linens have a character that is impossible to copy authentically but can be recreated, giving new household items an heirloom quality. Old samplers that have faded and mellowed with time have a particular charm that can be mimicked by matching the subtle colourings of the worn threads and fabrics, while tea is used to 'age' new linen.

1 Choose ivory and natural linen and cotton fabrics to achieve the best results.
2 Wash the fabric to remove any dressing that might have been applied to its surface during manufacture.
3 Make a pot of tea and leave it to brew in the usual way.
4 When the tea is cold, strain the liquid into a bowl and insert the linen. Soak for about 10 minutes, stirring occasionally.
5 Allow the fabric to drip dry naturally and iron out any creases before you begin to stitch.

Finished samplers can be treated in the same way to take any harshness away from the colours of threads and background fabric, but you will require a strong nerve when the stitched piece has taken a long time to work. Experiment first with a spare piece of background fabric worked with a few stitches.

Tea-dip ageing is only really suitable for decorative pieces that will not require washing. Make sure that all threads used are colourfast before attempting to use this technique!

Stretching and framing samplers and pictures

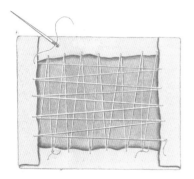

Before the finished work is framed it needs to be stretched over a piece of card to hold it flat and taut. A professional framer will be able to do this for you, but it is quite easy to do it yourself and will be considerably cheaper.

You will need a piece of acid-free board over which to stretch the work. This should be the same size as the design, plus an allowance for a narrow plain border all around the design for the frame rebate.

1 Iron the work on the wrong side, as described in Caring for your work, above.
2 The backing card needs to be the same size as the glass.
3 Cut the card and place to the wrong side of the sampler.

4 Fold the fabric over the card so that the embroidered area is centred.
5 Lace the back together with strong thread to hold it firmly in place.
6 Sew the long sides first, checking the final position, then work the short sides.

In the bedroom

Hand-stitched bedlinen is always a delight, both to see, and to use. Amongst this collection of beautiful bedlinen, you will find a wide collection of pretty designs to suit a variety of tastes. The simple cot blanket with nursery motifs, to make for a special baby, is an ideal choice for the novice as it is worked freehand in a slightly thicker thread. The experienced and competent embroiderer might appreciate something more elaborate to stitch, and the beautiful sheet turnback will offer this opportunity. An intricate, floral pattern, worked in a wide colour range, makes this a delicate addition to any bedroom.

Alternatively, a simple motif combined with a monogrammed initial, adds special style and individuality to the Oxford pillowcases.

sheet turnback

A verdant border of cottage-garden roses makes a splendid edging for a sheet turnback. Such dense stitching requires patience and experience, but the result is well worth the effort – transforming an everyday item into an heirloom. The turnback is designed to drape across the top of the bed and is not attached to the sheet, so it will require less laundering than the rest of the bedlinen and this will help to keep the embroidery in good condition. A heavy lace crocheted edging balances well with the strength and vibrancy of the floral design. You may even be lucky and find antique lace that is in good enough condition to use. The border is stitched from the centre outwards, so can be made to fit any size of bed.

About the turnback

Approximate finished size: 198 x 104cm
    (78 x 41in), excluding lace edging
Size of one motif: 34 wide x 18.5cm high
    (13½ x 7¼in)
Number of stitches per 2.5cm (1in): 14
Work stitches over two threads at a time
    when using a fabric with double the
    thread count

You will need

2.2m (2½yd) white linen, 140cm (55in)
    wide, 28 threads per 2.5cm (1in)
2m (2yd) lace edging
Tapestry needle size 24 or 26
Stranded cotton in the colours specified
    on pages 24–25.
Use two strands of thread throughout.

To work the design

1 Mark the position for the placement of the centre motif in the following way: fold the fabric in half widthways, and make a row of tacking stitches along the fold line to mark the centre, following the line of the warp threads.
2 Measure 18cm (7in) in from the edge of the fabric and make a short row of tacking stitches, following the line of the weft threads, to intersect the centre fold line. This line marks the position of the bottom of the border. Count 102 threads and make another row of tacking stitches, following the weft threads: this new line marks the top edge of the border.
3 Matching the centre line marked on the chart to the line of tacking along the centre of the fabric, work the first motif.
4 Working outwards from the centre, continue to stitch the rest of the border design until five motifs have been com-pleted (two either side of the centre one). If you have altered the size of the border, you will also need to adjust the number of motifs worked, and not the distance between them.
5 Work another half motif at either end of the border.

To make up

1 Trim the fabric to size. First, measure 12.5cm (5in) down from the bottom of the border, mark with pins and cut the fabric straight following the line of the weft threads. Next, measure 75cm (31¼in) up from the top of the border, mark with pins and cut the fabric, follow-ing the line of the weft threads. For the side edges, measure 101cm (40in) out both ways from the centre fold line, mark with pins and cut the fabric, following the line of the warp threads.
2 Press a 1cm (⅜in) turning to the wrong side along the bottom edge, then turn a 2.5cm (1in) hem. Stitch in position either by hand or by machine. If you wish, you can work a decorative drawn thread work hem, following the technique shown on page 18. This will give a more elegant finish to the turnback.
3 Make 1cm (⅜in) turnings, followed by 1cm (⅜in) hems, along the other three sides of the turnback. Stitch them in posi-tion, mitring the corners if required (see page 18).
4 Pin the lace edging all along the edge of the bottom hem, then tack and slip-stitch it neatly in place to complete the sheet turnback.
5 Press the turnback lightly on the wrong side to complete taking care not to squash the stitches.

Thread colours

		Anchor	DMC				Anchor	DMC
☐	cream	366	739			red	46	666
☐	yellow	301	745			rose	75	962
	peach	9	352			magenta	89	917
	rust	1049	3826			pale lilac	108	210

		Anchor	DMC			Anchor	DMC			Anchor	DMC
	lilac	109	209		blue	187	3814		brown	358	801
	purple	98	553		pale green	244	987		black	403	310
	dark purple	101	550		leaf-green	188	943				
	pale blue	186	993		bottle- green	683	890				

square bed cushions

Big and luxurious bed cushions make a decorative feature in a room, as well as providing a comfortable back rest for reading or breakfasting in bed. The cross stitch designs for both these cushions are made up of square motifs, worked in sequence to build up dense areas of colourful pattern on to a linen background. This type of patterning offers plenty of scope for adaptation and variation; you can arrange the same motifs in many different ways: for example, they could be worked in rows around the cushion, to create deeper borders, or alternated, to make a chequerboard effect. For a classic finishing touch, the cushions are fastened at the back with pearl buttons.

About the cushions

Star cushion (pages 28–29)
Approximate size: 71cm (28in) square
Number of stitches per 2.5cm (1in): 11
Flower cushion (pages 30–31)
Approximate size: 62cm (24½in) square
Number of stitches per 2.5cm (1in): 18
Work the stitches over two threads at a
    time when using fabric with double
    the thread count.

Star cushion

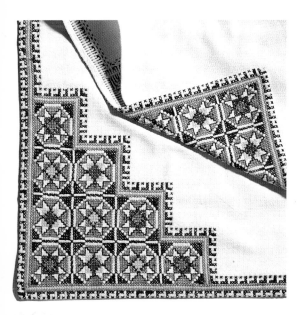

You will need

1.7m (1¾yd) antique white Hardanger, 140cm (55in) wide, 22 threads per 2.5cm (1in)

6 pearl buttons, 2cm (¾in) in diameter

Cushion pad, 71cm (21in) square approximately

Tapestry needle size 24 or 26

Stranded cotton in the colours specified

Use two strands of thread throughout

To work the design

1 For the cushion front, cut a piece of fabric 87cm (33in) square. Position the central diamond pattern by folding the fabric in half, lengthways then widthways. Mark the folds with rows of tacking stitches that cross at the centre point. Follow the line of the fabric threads.

2 Matching the centre point marked on the chart to the centre point marked on the fabric, work the diamond arrange-ment of star motifs as placed, following the colour chart until it is complete. Where indicated on the chart, work back-stitch outline stitches (see page 15) around the motifs.

3 Leaving a band of plain fabric, 8cm (3½in) wide all round, begin at one cor-ner and work the narrow border pattern, followed by the corner blocks of star motifs as shown on the chart.

4 Trim the cushion front to size, leaving a seam allowance of 1.5cm (⅝in) on each side. The cushion front should now mea-sure 74cm (29¼in) square.

To make up

1 For the cushion back, cut two rectan-gles of fabric: a small one measuring 74 x 26cm (29¼ x 10¼in) and a large one measuring 74 x 65.5cm (29¼ x 26in).

2 Make up the cushion following the instructions on page 30.

Thread colours

		Anchor	DMC
	pink	76	961
	yellow	289	307
	green	257	905
	blue	164	824
	black	403	310

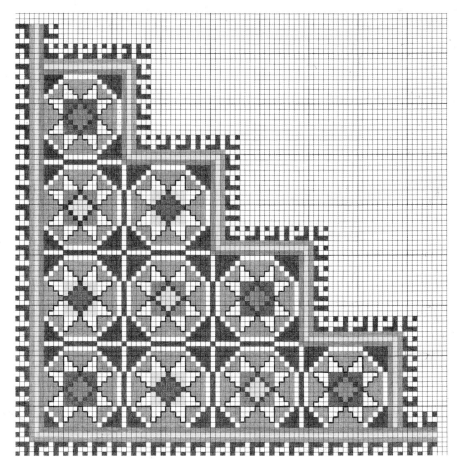

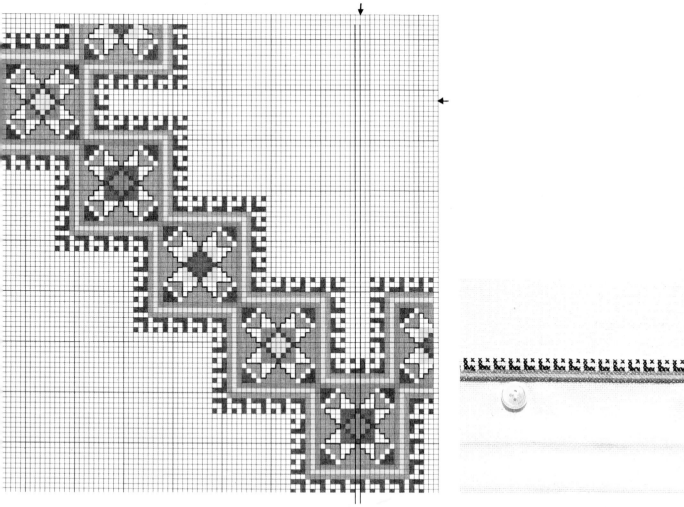

This detail of the cushion back shows the hemmed button band.

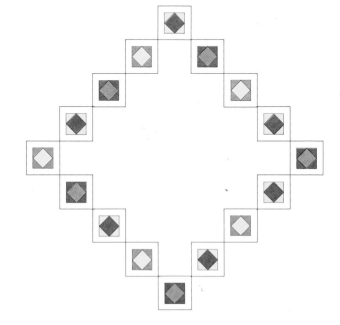

Flower cushion

You will need

1.5m (1¾yd) antique white Edinburgh linen, 140cm (55in) wide, 36 threads per 2.5cm (1in)

6 pearl buttons, 2cm (¾in) diameter

Cushion pad, 62cm (24.5in) square approximately

Tapestry needle size 24 or 26

Stranded cotton in the colours specified on pages 32–33

Use two strands of thread throughout

To work the design

1 Cut a piece of fabric 78cm (29½in) square for the cushion front. Mark the centre of each side by folding the fabric, and then work a line approximately 20cm (8in) long, of tacking stitches, at right angles to the edges of the fabric.

2 Leaving a 9cm (4in) edge of fabric all the way around the outside, begin at one corner and, working outwards, stitch the narrow border pattern. Work first in one direction to the centre of one side, then in the other direction to the centre of the other side, following the line of the fabric threads. Work from the other three corners in the same way until the border is completed all around the cushion. The bud patterns slant diagonally in towards the centre. Make any adjustments necessary where the borders meet.

3 Next, work the corner motifs within the border, following the chart.

4 Then work the arrangement of three motifs, placing them centrally along each side of the cushion. Work backstitch outline stitches (see page 15) around motifs as indicated on the chart.

5 Trim the front to size, leaving a 1cm (⅜in) band of unstitched fabric all around the embroidered border, plus a seam allowance of 1.5cm (⅝in) on all sides. The cushion front should now measure 65cm (25¾in) square.

To make up

1 For the cushion back, cut a rectangle of fabric 65 x 26cm (25¾ x 10¼in) and another one 65 x 56.5cm (25¾ x 22½in).

2 Make up the cushion following the instructions below.

3 Decorate the edge of the cushion with closely worked rows of blanket stitch (see page 15) or work a narrow border of crochet if preferred.

To make up the finished cushions

Make up the cushions after the designs have been worked on to the fronts. Both cushions are made up in the same way.

1 Prepare the pieces for the back of the cushion. Taking the smaller rectangle, make a hem along one long side, making turnings of 1.5cm (⅝in) then 5cm (2in). Tack in position, press, then stitch by hand or machine.

2 Cut and stitch six buttonholes along this hem. Start by marking the holes at each end, 8cm (3in) in from the side, then space the remaining four evenly between them. Work the buttonholes by hand or alternatively using a sewing machine. Make sure that they are big enough to fit the buttons.

3 Hem along one long edge of the large rectangle for the back, making turnings of 1cm (⅜in) then 2cm (¾in). Tack in position, press and then stitch together by hand or machine.

4 With right sides together, place the small rectangle on to the cushion front, matching raw edges along three sides, and pin in place. Position the larger rectangle on to the cushion front in the same way, matching raw edges and ensuring that the hemmed edge overlaps that of the small rectangle. Pin and tack.

5 Stitch around the seams, within the seam allowance and following the grain of the fabric, trim the corners and turn to the right side. Press the edges carefully, taking care not to squash the embroidery.

6 Sew on the buttons to complete.

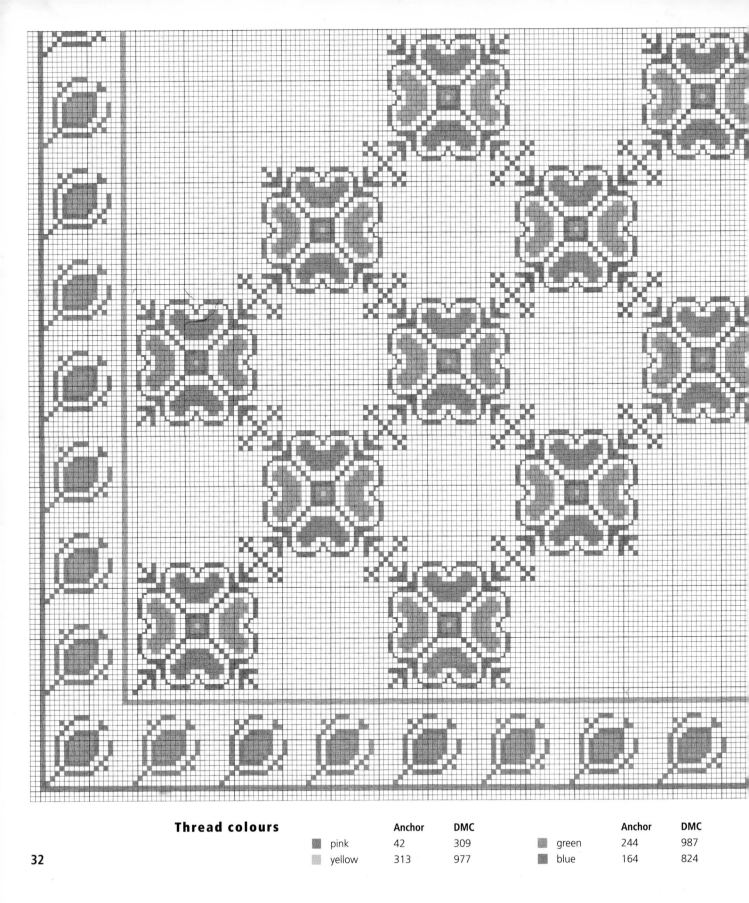

Thread colours

		Anchor	DMC			Anchor	DMC
	pink	42	309		green	244	987
	yellow	313	977		blue	164	824

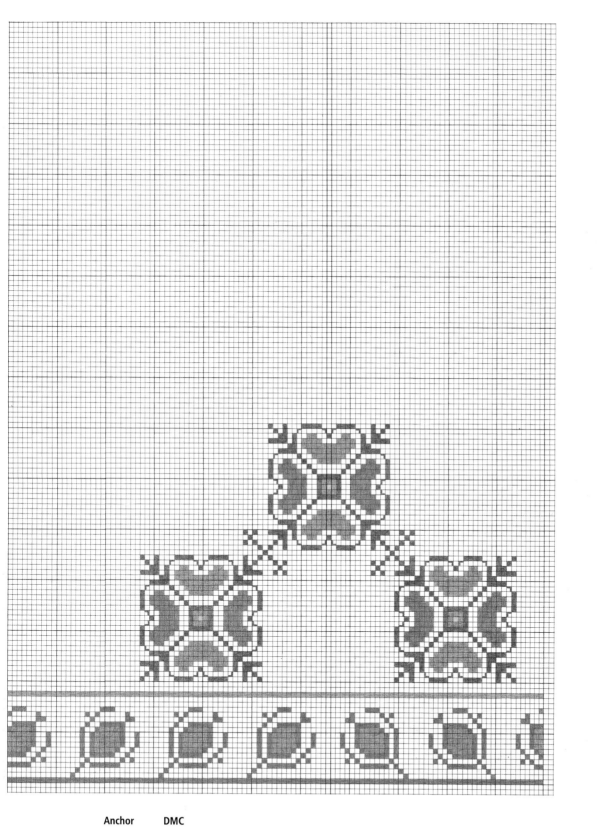

		Anchor	DMC
▨	brown	905	3781

monogrammed pillowcases

Traditional embroidered monograms add a distinctive flourish to household linens. Worked on waste canvas, they can be sewn directly on to existing bedlinen or attached as a complete motif on to cotton or linen fabric; as they require only a small amount of stitching, they are an ideal project for the novice stitcher. Oxford pillowcases have a classic style, providing a perfect foil for monograms, and they are surprisingly simple to make. Draw out your own monogram following the charted alphabets on pages 98–101; use graph tracing paper to position intertwined letters with elegant sweeping curves linking them together. Alternatively, why not work an alphabet together with a motif such as crowns or keys, as shown in the charts on page 105, to give your linen regal appeal.

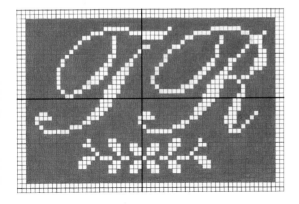

Thread colour

	Anchor	DMC
cream	926	822

About the pillowcases

Approximate finished size: 91 x 66cm (36 x 26in), including 8cm (3¼in) border
Number of stitches per 2.5cm (1in): 10

You will need

For one pillowcase:
2.1m (1¼yd) cotton chambray, 112cm (44in) wide
Waste canvas, 10 threads per 2.5cm (1in)
Crewel needle size 7
Stranded cotton in the colour below
Use three strands of thread throughout

To prepare the fabric and work the design

1 For the front, cut a piece of chambray 94 x 69cm (37 x 27in), following the grain of the fabric. Tack the stitching line for the inside border edge, 9.5cm (3⅝in) from the edges of the fabric and parallel to all four sides of the rectangle. For the back, cut two pieces of fabric: the main piece 84.5 x 69cm (33 x 27in) and the flap 35.5 x 69cm (15½ x 27in).

2 Draw your monogram on graph paper, following the charted alphabets on pages 98-101, and mark the centre point by drawing two intersecting lines. Cut a piece of waste canvas, following the threads; make it 5cm (2½in) bigger than the monogram on every side and mark the horizontal and vertical centre threads lightly with pencil.

3 For a centrally placed monogram, mark the centre point on the pillowcase front with two lines of intersecting tacking stitches (see page 16) or place the monogram elsewhere on the pillowcase, such as a corner, marking the position with

tacking stitches running straight or diagonally, as required, to correspond to the horizontal and vertical intersecting lines marked on the chart.

4 Tack the waste canvas in place, matching the pencil lines to the tacking stitches on the fabric. Work the monogram from the chart, plotting the letters from the centre outwards.

5 When stitching is complete, remove the waste canvas threads carefully (see page 17). Press the work lightly.

To make up

1 Making turnings of 2cm (¾in) then 3cm (1½in), turn under a hem to the wrong side along one short edge of the main back piece. Tack and press, then stitch in place. In the same way, turn under a hem to the wrong side of one long edge on the flap piece, making turnings of 1cm (⅜in) then 2cm (¾in).

2 With right sides together, place the back flap on the pillowcase front, matching raw edges along three of the sides. Place the main back piece on to the pillowcase front in the same way as before, so that the hemmed edge of the pillowcase overlaps the hemmed edge of the flap, being sure to match raw edges. Pin and tack all around.

3 Stitch around the pillowcase, taking a 1.5cm (⅝in) seam allowance. Trim the corners and turn the pillowcase to the right side, then tack close to the outside edge and press. Measure and then machine stitch a line 8cm (3in) from all edges to make the border.

4 Remove the tacking stitches and carefully press on the wrong side.

cot blanket

An embroidered blanket, decorated with simple motifs, makes a charming cot cover. Old blankets can be cut to size and bound with blanket stitches in a coloured thread, giving them a new lease of life; brand-new blankets work just as well. Choose a classic colour and make sure the wool is soft. A simple grid, made from lines worked in freehand cross stitches, divides the blanket into squares, into which the motifs are placed. Work as few, or as many motifs as you like, to make the project simple or more ambitious. Use the number and alphabet motifs shown on pages 98–101, to cover a bigger blanket for a child's bed.

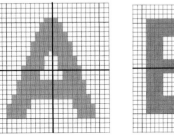
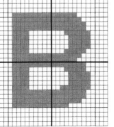

Thread colours

		Anchor	DMC
	coral	10	2356
	blue	168	2826
	dark blue	161	2797
	pink	24	2818
	yellow	293	2743
	lime	0278	2218
	pale green	185	2599
	tan	362	2158
	beige	392	2642

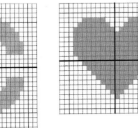

About the blanket

Approximate finished size: 76 x109cm
  (30 x 43in)
Number of stitches per 2.5cm (1in): 8.5

You will need

0.8m x 113cm (32 x 45in) blanket fabric
Waste canvas, 8.5 threads per 2.5cm (1in)
Tapestry needle size 20 or 22
Soft embroidery cotton in the colours
  specified left
Use one strand of thread throughout

To prepare the blanket

1 Along each edge of the blanket, make hems by rolling up 1cm (⅜in) of fabric, twice. Tack in place. Using soft embroidery cotton, which has a matt finish and is available in a large range of colours, work blanket stitch (see page 15) all around the blanket edges. Make each stitch large enough to cover the depth of the hem and hold it in place.
2 Divide the width of the blanket into five equal parts and, placing pins at regular intervals, mark four lines down the length of it. Tack beside the pins to mark the lines then remove the pins. Work even lines of cross stitches over the tacked lines, then remove the tacking.

3 Divide the length of the blanket into seven equal parts and use pins to mark six lines. Tack, then work cross stitch as in step 2, to form a grid of squares over the whole blanket. Remove the tacking.

To work the motifs

Following the charts, work the motifs centrally within the squares, (see pictures). Proceed as follows:
1 Cut the waste canvas into 11cm (4½in) squares and following the line of the threads, lightly mark the central lines with a pencil in both directions.
2 Mark the centre of the square to be worked with two lines of tacking stitches. Place a piece of waste canvas on to the square, matching the centre markings, and tack it in place. Choose a motif from the charts and, plotting it from the centre outwards, stitch it over the canvas, following the chart.
3 Remove the waste canvas carefully (see page 17), leaving the embroidered shapes in the squares.

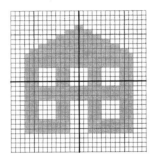
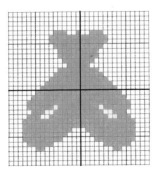
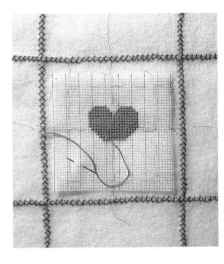

For the table

The selection of designs in this chapter offers something to suit all tastes. Beautifully embroidered tablelinens set the style, and are always a useful item to make. Choose classic rose motifs evoking an English summer's day or, alternatively, a blue and white traditional cross stitch design, reminiscent of Dutch tile work. For lunch al fresco or cosy supper parties, the gingham tablemats are a perfect choice. They are decorated with snowflake medallions, which are worked in groups of crosses forming colourful patterns over the gingham squares; a selection of alternative medallion motifs is provided enabling you to work a different one on every mat if you wish. Add the finishing touch to any well-dressed table with the original numbered napkin rings, which will appeal to those who enjoy rather quicker results.

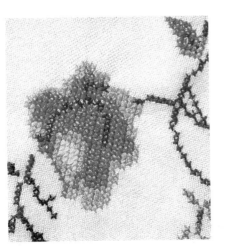

rose tablecloth

Rose flowers and buds are classic motifs, instantly conjuring up the delights of summer gardens and luxuriant arbours, clad with fragrant blooms. When decorated with rose patterns in cross stitch, tablelinens will impart a cottage-like atmosphere to your home. They also make the perfect setting for pretty, floral china, both for afternoon tea and informal dining. The cloth shown here can be adapted to fit any size of table by simply adding more motifs around the edges to suit your own requirements. You will find that the motifs which decorate the border are easy to work. It is worth making up the cloth properly before you start to work the cross stitch, as the hemmed edges will prevent the fabric from fraying while stitching is in progress. If looked after well, a fine tablecloth such as this is destined to become a family heirloom.

About the tablecloth

Approximate finished size: 140cm (55in) square

Number of stitches per 2.5cm (1in): 11

Work stitches over two threads at a time when using fabric with double the thread count

You will need

1.5m 1¾(yd) evenweave linen, 150cm (59in) wide, 22 threads per 2.5cm (1in)

Tapestry needle size 24 or 26

Stranded cotton in the colours specified on page 42

Use two strands of thread throughout

To prepare the fabric

1 Cut the fabric to 145cm (57in) square. Make a hem all round by turning under 1cm (⅜in) then 1.5cm (⅝in). Mitre each corner (see page 18). Pin and tack the hem in position.

2 Secure the hem with slipstitch, then remove the tacking.

3 With right sides facing, work cross stitches all around the edge of the cloth so that, at the back, the cross stitches catch the top edge of the hem.

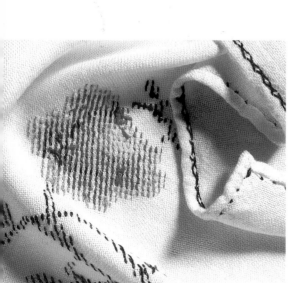

To work the design

1 Measure 13cm (5in) in from the edges of the cloth, making a square. Mark with pins, then work lines of tacking stitches. This defines the outer edge of the border.

2 Fold the square in half and, using the fold lines, mark the centre points on two of the sides with a few tacking stitches.

Unfold and repeat for the other sides. Matching the edge line on the chart to the tacked border line, work a flower and bud motif on the marked centre of each side of the border square.

3 Work a flower and bud motif at each corner, inside the border lines. Position the motif as on the chart, matching the edge and corner lines to the tacked lines on the tablecloth.

4 Halve the space between the motifs and mark with tacking stitches. Work a long border motif between each flower and bud, matching the edge and central lines on the chart to the tacked lines and centre markings. Remove the tacking.

41

5 Fold the tablecloth into quarters to find the centre point and mark it with a pin. Measure 26cm (10½in) out from the centre point along each fold, and again mark with pins. Using the pin markers as a guide, work straight lines of tacking stitches to make a 52cm (21in) square in the centre of the cloth. Leave the pins in place for now.

6 Work a flower and bud motif at each corner of this smaller square, placing them so as to match the edge and corner lines on the chart to the tacked lines. Work a short border motif between the flower and bud motifs, matching the edge line to the tacked line, and the centre line to the pin markers. Remove the pins and the tacking stitches.

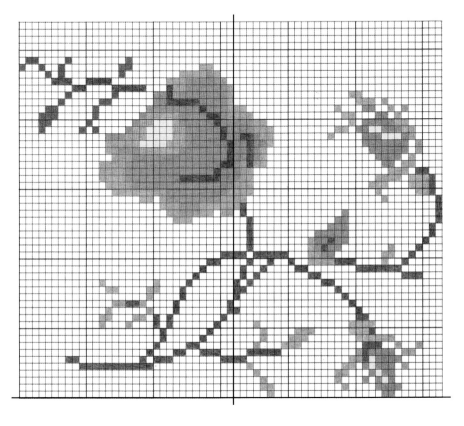

Thread colours

		Anchor	DMC
	red	9046	321
	pink	54	956
	yellow	288	445
	brown	381	938
	dark green	212	561
	bright green	255	907
	royal	134	820

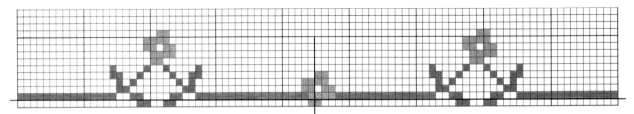

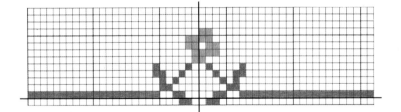

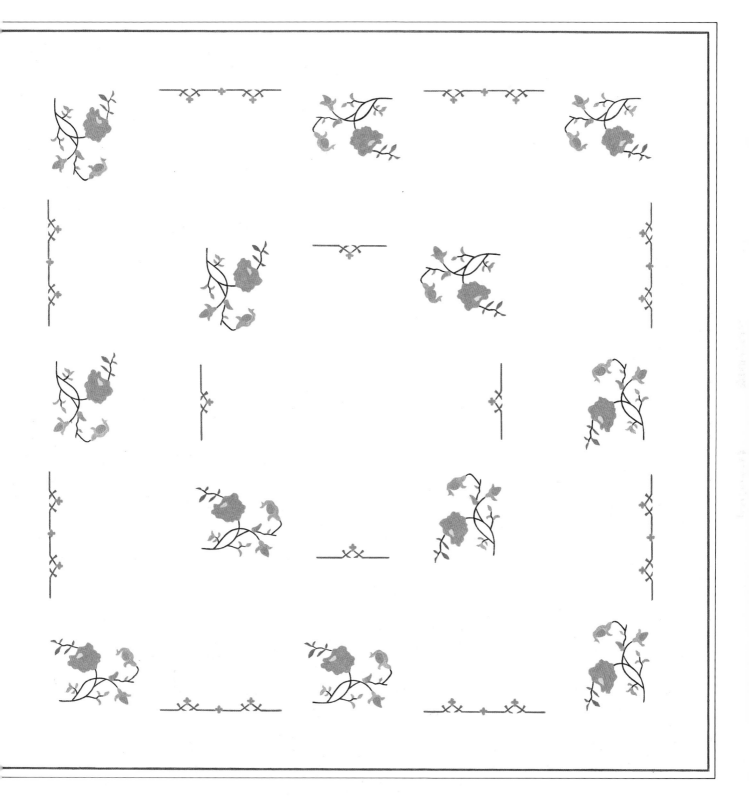

blue and white tablecloth

Blue and white brings a freshness to traditional cross stitch designs and is an ideal colour combination for tablelinens. Patterns made up of square motifs are versatile and relatively easy to work. Here, an antique cloth has two alternating motifs – a flower and a geometric square – filling each corner. The centre panel is decorated with a delicate, open grid.

The original piece was worked with great skill by an experienced stitcher using fine woollen crêpe fabric; for the less experienced a fine linen, on which the threads are easy to count, is recommended, making the overall effect easier to achieve. Alternatively, the design can be simplified by working on a fabric with a lower thread count, resulting in larger blocks of pattern which will fill the cloth much more quickly.

About the tablecloth

Approximate finished size: 99 x 108cm
    (39 x 42½in)
Number of stitches per 2.5cm (1in): 16
Work stitches over two threads at a time
    when using fabric with double the
    thread count

You will need

1.2m (1½yd) evenweave linen, 140cm
    (55in) wide, 32 threads per 2.5cm (1in)
Tapestry needle size 24
Stranded cotton in the colours specified
    on pages 46–47
Use two strands of thread throughout

To work the design

1 Starting from one corner of the fabric, measure 20cm (8in) in from the long edge and 15cm (6in) in from the short edge; mark the fabric with a pin, setting the first corner point. Make lines of tacking stitches from this point, following the grain of the fabric, thus marking the outer edges for the positioning of the blocks of motifs along two sides of the tablecloth – one short, one long.

2 Beginning in the corner marked out by tacking stitches and starting with a square motif, stitch 27 alternating flower and square motifs in a row, inside the line of tacking, along the longer side (see charts). Stitch the flowers facing in towards the centre of the cloth.

3 Starting from the square motif in the corner, work 11 alternating flower and square motifs in a row, inside the line of tacking, along the shorter edge (see charts). Leave a gap of six threads then, beginning with a flower motif, work a

further 12 motifs, to take you to the next corner point.

4 To complete the border, work rows of motifs on the other two sides of the rectangle to match the two sides already stitched. Fill in the corners with diagonal rows of alternating motifs. Fewer rows of motifs can be worked if required.

5 Fold the cloth into quarters, matching the edges of the rectangle made up of square motifs, and use a pin to mark the centre point within the patterned area. Work a square motif at the centre of the cloth. Following the chart (see pages 46–47), plot out the flower and leaf border design so that it forms a grid around the centrally placed motif. Work a square motif in the middle of the eight other spaces made by the grid.

6 Starting from the corner work towards the middle stitching the outer border pattern around the cloth. Where the stitching meets along the sides, make any adjustments necessary to fit the pattern.

To make up

1 Measure 3.5cm (1¼in) from the outside edges of the border on all sides and cut the fabric, following the grain.

2 Turn under hems of 5mm (¼in) followed by 1cm (⅜in) along the long sides of the cloth, tack and press. Make drawn thread work hems (see page 18) along both sides.

3 In the same way, turn under hems along the short sides of the cloth and make drawn thread work hems. The drawn thread work hems make the corners into decorative squares; mitring is not required.

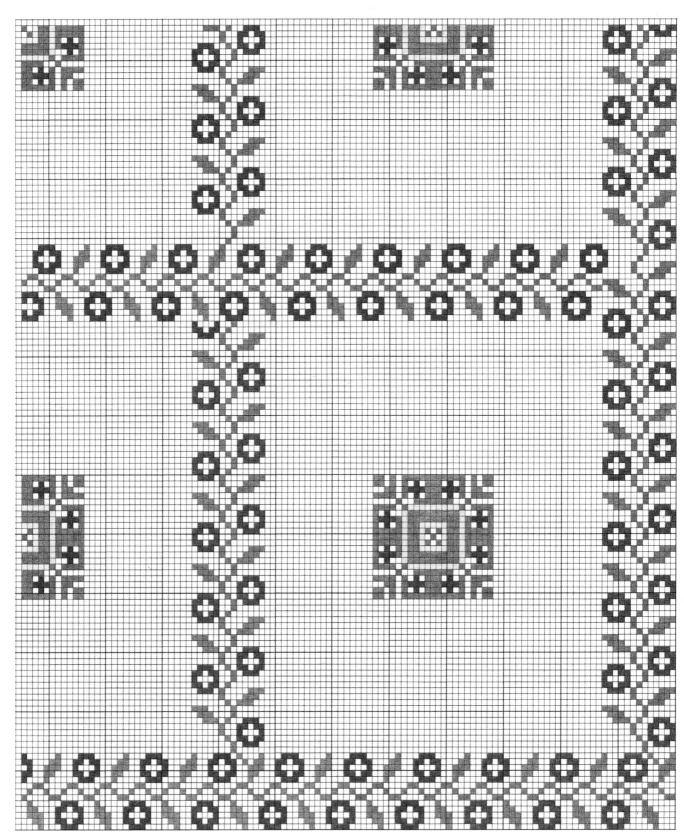

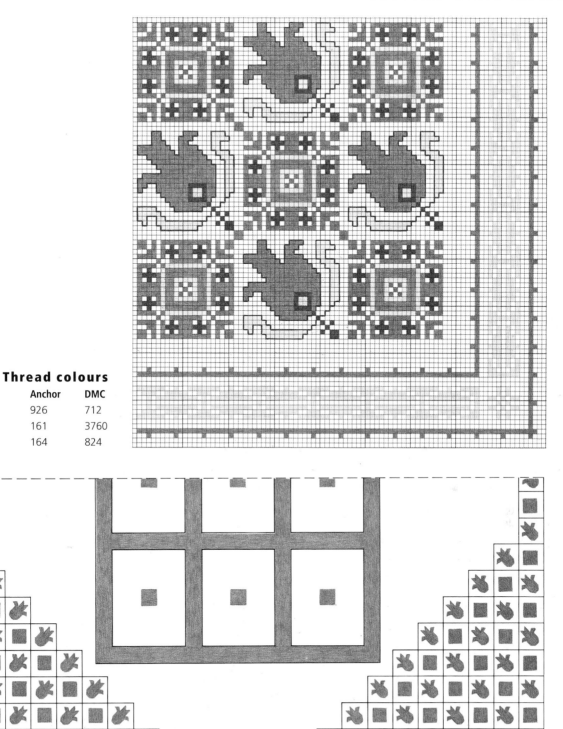

Thread colours

		Anchor	DMC
	cream	926	712
	blue	161	3760
	navy	164	824

gingham tablemats

Gingham is always popular and comes in a large range of bright and attractive colours. The checks can be used to provide a background ideal for plotting cross stitch patterns. Depending on the size of the squares, one stitch can be worked over a single tiny square or, on a larger scale within a bigger square, four or five stitches can be used to make a symmetrical pattern.

Tablemats made from gingham are a perfect project for the beginner. Choose a gingham with a similar pattern to the one shown in the pictures and remember to adapt the design to suit your fabric by drawing the medallion snowflake pattern (below) on graph paper. Consider the placement of motifs before cutting the fabric and make any necessary adjustments to the size of the mats at this stage. Charts for alternative medallion motifs are shown on pages 108–109.

About the tablemats

Approximate finished size: 41 x 31cm
    (16 x 12¼in), excluding trimming
Number of stitches per 2.5cm (1in): 12

You will need

For each mat:
44 x 34cm (17¼ x 13½in) gingham
Backing fabric and interlining, cut to the
    same dimensions as the gingham
70cm (27in) trimming or braid
Crewel needle size 7
Stranded cotton in the colours specified
    below
Use two strands of thread throughout

To work the design

1 Working from the chart, stitch the medallion motifs to fill the large gingham squares, working a single cross stitch into each of the smaller squares on the fabric. Arrange the motifs on to the tablemat to your own liking.

To make up

1 Along the short edges of both the gingham and the backing fabric, turn under and press 1.5cm (⅝in) to the wrong side. Cut off 1.5cm (⅝in) of the interlining fabric along both of the short edges. Place the interlining on the wrong side of the gingham, matching long edges, and folding the short side edge turnings over the interlining to enclose the raw edges. Tack together the interlining and the gingham.
2 With right sides facing, pin the backing fabric to the gingham along the long sides. Machine stitch the long sides, taking seam allowances of 1.5cm (⅝in), to make a tube. Turn the tube to the right side and press the seams open, taking care not to flatten any cross stitches.
3 Pin and tack the turned side edges together, then slipstitch. Stitch a length of trimming or braid in place over both side edges.

Thread colours

		Anchor	DMC
☐	yellow	278	472
■	blue	148	311
▨	rust	339	920

numbered napkin rings

Numbered napkin rings add a special touch to everyday dining and entertaining. House guests can be allotted their own personal napkin ring, for their sole use throughout the time of their stay. The cross stitch numbers are worked over waste canvas, making the stitches easy to count. Quick to stitch, they add a stylish embellishment to classic moiré napkin rings. Choose a decorative button or bead to fasten with the loop at the back and ring the changes by stitching a monogram, choosing the letter from one of the alphabets (see 98–101). You could make a set of these quite quickly as an unusual gift.

About the napkin rings

Approximate finished size: 20 x 5cm (8 x 2in), fastening to give a diameter of approximately 5cm (2in)

Number of stitches per 2.5cm (1in): 12

You will need

For each napkin ring:

50cm (20in), of moiré grosgrain ribbon 5cm (2in) wide

Waste canvas, 12 threads per 2.5cm (1in)

Buckram

Buttons or beads

Crewel needle size 7

Stranded cotton in the colours specified below

Use two strands of thread throughout

To work the design

1 Fold the ribbon in half widthways, marking the fold with tacking stitches. With the right side of the ribbon facing, measure 15.5cm (6¼in) out from the fold towards one end of the ribbon. Mark this point with a line of tacking stitches across the width of the ribbon to position the cross stitch number.

2 Cut a piece of waste canvas 7cm (2½in) square, pin it centrally over the marked line, then tack it in place. Working from the chart, stitch a number, through both the waste canvas and the ribbon. Alternatively, stitch a letter instead (see pages 98–101).

3 Once the stitching is complete, remove the waste canvas threads carefully (see page 17).

To make up

1 Measure 21cm (8⅜in) in each direction from the tacked centre fold line. Cut the piece of ribbon straight across the width at both ends.

2 With right sides together, fold one end of the ribbon lengthways, so that the selvedges meet. Pin and stitch along the raw edge, taking a seam allowance of 1cm (⅜in). Trim the corner close to the seam, press the seam open and turn to the right side to make a pointed end. Finish the other end of the ribbon in the same way.

3 With wrong sides together, fold the ribbon in half so that the two pointed ends match exactly. Cut a shaped piece of buckram to fit the folded ribbon. Tack it in place, tacking through all the layers together to keep them firm. Slipstitch all the way along the edges so as to encase the piece of buckram.

4 Roll the napkin ring to give an overlap of approximately 2cm (¾in) and either stitch it in place or make a loop fastening. Sew on the button or bead fastening to complete the napkin.

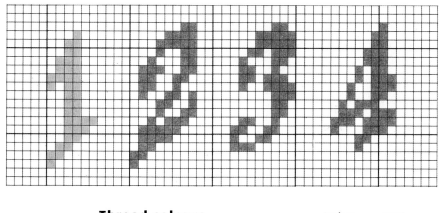

Thread colours

		Anchor	DMC
	lilac	870	3042
	gold	363	436
	pink	77	3350
	green	878	501

In the sitting room

Hand-worked pieces add an individual touch in the sitting room and these designs range from the traditional to the very contemporary. The samplers and cushion have been copied from original designs, and adapted to fit a modern home, without losing any of their simplicity and charm.

The director's chairs become stylish pieces of furniture with their covers embellished with a striking crown or heart motif. A soft woollen throw with a pretty cross stitch border will disguise an old sofa, or you could simply make the same ribbon border to edge a blanket to take with you on a picnic by the river on a hot summer's day.

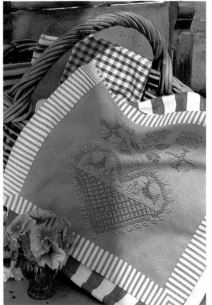

director's chair cover

Director's chairs have classic looks and simple lines that fit into almost any home or garden with perfect ease. They also have the practical advantage of folding flat, so they can be stored away when not in use. The covers are put together inside out over each chair, making it possible to adapt them to fit any chair. The cross stitch crown and heart motifs, which are worked directly on to the cover in pearl cotton, have a wonderful embossed texture; alternatively, the motif can be made up on to a square of fabric which can then be appliquéd to a finished chair cover.

About the chair cover

Cover fits a standard director's-style chair, with flat-topped wooden arms

Size of each completed motif:
Crown: 21 x 25cm (8¼ x10in);
Heart: 18 x 27cm (7 x 10½in)
Number of stitches per 2.5cm (1in): 11

You will need

3.1m (3½yd) Indian cotton fabric, 112cm (48in) wide

Waste canvas, approximately 40cm (15½in) square, 11 threads per 2.5cm (1in)

Crewel needle size 6

Pearl cotton in the colours specified on pages 56–57

Pattern paper or tailor's chalk

To cut out

1 Make a paper pattern for the cover using the dimensions of the chair, taken as described in the steps opposite. Each set of measurements makes a rectangular or square pattern piece (see diagram). Sketch it on to paper first and then make a pattern to size before cutting out the fabric. Allow an extra 8cm (3in) on each side for seams and hems; this generous seam allowance can be trimmed down later, after the cover has been made up. If you feel confident, you could draw directly on to the wrong side of the fabric with tailor's chalk, adding a seam allowance as above. Where two pieces are needed (see step 7), remember to reverse the pattern if the shape is irregular.

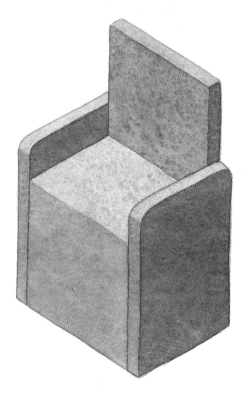

2 For the main piece (A), starting at floor level at the lower-back edge, measure up and over the chair, back down to the seat, then across the seat and down the front to the floor. This makes the long side of a rectangle. For the short side, measure the width of the seat (front edge and back), and the width of the chair, both at the top of the chair back and at floor level (front and back). Follow step 1 to make a pattern for piece A.

3 For the side panels (B), measure the dimensions along the floor (from front to back), along the top of the chair arm (front to back), and from the floor to the top of the chair arm at the front and at the back. Follow step 1 to make a pattern for piece B.

4 For the inside arms (C), measure the length of the chair arm, from where it meets the chair back to the front, the depth of the seat, and the distance (back and front) from the seat to the top of the arm. Follow step 1 to make a pattern for piece C.

5 For the arm gusset (D), start at the front of the chair and measure from the floor up to the front of the chair arm, along the top of the arm to the back of the chair, then down to the floor at the back. Measure the width of the chair arm. Follow step 1 to make a pattern for piece D.

6 For the side gussets (E), measure from the top of the arm at the back of the chair, to the top of the chair back, then measure the width of the wooden struts supporting the canvas chair back. Follow step 1 to make a pattern for piece E.

7 Pin the pattern pieces to the fabric, following the grain. Cut: 1 main piece (A), 2 side panels (B), 2 inside arms (C), 2 arm gussets (D) and 2 side gussets (E). Tack a line across the width of the main piece (A) to mark the top of the chair back and to use for the positioning of the cross stitch motif as described on page 56.

Key

A   Main piece (back, front)
B   Side panels
C   Inside arms
D   Arm gussets
E   Side gussets

A

B
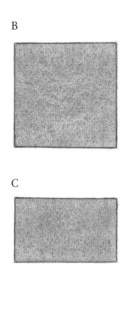

C

D   E

To work the design

1 The motif is stitched on to the back of main piece (A) before the chair cover is made up. Position the motif by folding the back of piece A in half lengthways, marking the fold with a line of tacking stitches, following the grain of the fabric. Work another line of tacking stitches running at right angles to the centre fold line, parallel to and 24cm (9½in) from the tacking line marking the top of the chair (see To cut out, step 7).

2 On the waste canvas, mark the central threads, running horizontally and vertically, then tack it in position on the right side of the fabric, matching the centre markings to those on the fabric.

3 Work the cross stitch motif over the waste canvas, following the charts and plotting the design from the centre out towards the edges.

4 When the stitching is complete, remove the waste canvas one thread at a time.

5 Alternatively, the motif can be made up on to a square of fabric which you can then appliqué to a finished chair cover (see page 58).

Thread colours

		Anchor	DMC			Anchor	DMC
■	lilac	0939	793	■	pale blue	0977	334
■	lightest blue	976	3325	■	mid blue	0978	322

Thread colours

		Anchor	DMC			Anchor	DMC
	pale gold	0887	422		gold	0888	420
	mid gold	0945	3046		lime	0278	472

To make up

1 Place the main piece (A), wrong side out, over the chair and pin side gussets (E), also wrong side out, in position on both sides. Make sure the back fits well over the chair but has some ease in it, so that when complete the seams are not strained and the cover is easily removed. Snip the seam allowance at the top corners on the main piece, to open around the top corners of the gusset. Remove the cover from the chair and sew the gussets in place, taking the seam allowance needed when pinned to fit.

2 Put the cover back on the chair, wrong side out, and pin the inside arm pieces (C) to the main piece (A), from the bottom of the side gussets, down to the seat, then along its outside edges. If they are irregular in shape, check each piece is in the correct place. Keep them in place along the top of the arm rests using sticky tape. Snip the seam allowances and sew the inside arms in place.

3 Put the cover back on the chair, wrong side out, and pin the arm gussets (D) in place up the front edges of the main piece (A) and inside arms (C), across the tops of the inside arms, along the bottoms of the side gussets (E), then down the side edges of the main piece at the back. Snip the seam allowances where necessary. Remove the cover from the chair and sew the arm gussets in place.

4 Put the cover back on the chair, wrong side out, and pin the side panels (B) along the edges of the arm gussets (D). Check that each piece is correctly placed. Snip seam allowances, remove from the chair and sew the side panels in place.

5 Press open the seams, trim away excess bulky fabric and neaten the edges.

6 Turn right side out and put in place over the chair. Turn under and pin a hem all around the bottom edge of the cover. Remove the cover from the chair and stitch the hem in place. Press to finish.

To appliqué the motif

If you prefer, you can buy a ready-made chair cover as shown on page 53, on which to appliqué the motif. We used a contrasting fabric for the backing square.

1 Cut a 28cm (11in) square of fabric. Position the design following the instructions on page 16.

2 Work the motif over the waste canvas, following the chart on page 56 plotting the design from the centre out towards the edges. Carefully remove the waste canvas (see page 17) to complete. Turn a small single hem and press.

3 For the contrasting border, measure and cut four strips of fabric, 10cm (4in) wide by the length of the hemmed square, plus an extra 10cm (4in) for mitring the corners. Fold the pieces in half along the width, mitre the corners (see page 18) and sew on to the square.

4 Appliqué the finished square to the back of a finished chair cover.

blue panel curtains

Embroidered panels add a lavish finishing touch to curtains in the sitting room. Cross stitch designs, worked in bands that run horizontally, can be used to make borders or to edge a heading on simple country curtains. The basic lines of a ticking stripe suit this style of decoration particularly well; the top, in contrasting ticking, forms an unusual soft, bunched heading when the curtains are drawn back.

The panels are worked separately and are then stitched on to the curtains before making up. This allows plenty of scope for different fabric combinations to co-ordinate with the patterned panels. Alternatively, for a plainer effect, the panel design can be worked directly on to a wide linen fabric to form the main body of the curtains.

About the curtains

Approximate finished size of each curtain:
   90cm (36in) long x 120cm (47in) wide
Size of one repeat pattern: 24 x 8cm
   (9½ x 3in)
Number of stitches per 2.5cm (1in): 12/13
Work stitches over two threads at a
   time when using fabric with double the
   thread count

Note

As a general guide, this style of curtain needs to be 1½–2 times the width of the window. Curtains made to the size given above will suit a window approximately 120–160cm (47–63in) wide by 90cm (36in) long. Adapt the measurements to fit your own windows.

You will need

For a pair of curtains:
30cm (½yd) evenweave linen, 140cm
   (55in) wide, 25 threads per 2.5cm (1in)
2.2m (2½yd) ticking fabric, 140cm (55in)
   wide
1m (1¼yd) contrasting fabric, 140cm
   (55in) wide (for the heading flap)
2.5m (2¾yd) of standard, gathered heading tape, 3cm (1¼in) wide
4 button weights
Tapestry needle size 24
Stranded cotton in the colour specified
   below
Use two strands of thread throughout

To work the design

1 Fold the linen in half lengthways and cut along the fold, following the grain of the fabric, to make two strips. Fold one of the strips in half again lengthways and mark the fold line with pins. Work a row of tacking stitches, following the grain of the fabric, to mark the centre line. Mark the second strip in the same way.

2 Beginning 3cm (1¼in) up from one end of one of the strips, begin to plot out the design, following the chart and placing the pattern centrally on the linen. Continue to work the panel until the required length has been completed. Work the second panel in the same way.

To make up

1 Cut the main fabric to make two equal sized pieces to the required length, allowing an extra 16cm (6in) at the bottom for the hem and 3cm (1¼in) at the top. Fold over a double hem, taking two turnings of 8cm (3in) each. Press and tack. Turn 9cm (3½in) to the wrong side on each side edge and catch the edges down with large herringbone stitches, ending 18cm (7in) above each bottom corner. Mitre the hem at each bottom corner and sew a button weight inside, then complete the herringbone stitching. Slipstitch the bottom hem in place.

2 For each cross stitch panel, trim the fabric to within 1cm (⅜in) of the stitching, then turn the edges to the wrong side, to the edge of the stitching, and tack. Position the panels on the curtain so the bottom edges of the panels are level with the hemline and there is a 10cm (4in) border of fabric along the inside edges, where the curtains will meet when drawn. Slipstitch the panels in place.

3 Cut two heading flaps, each measuring 140 x 46cm (55 x 18½in). Turn under 9cm (3½in) to the wrong side on each of

Thread colours

		Anchor	DMC
▨	blue	169	806

the short side edges. Hold firm with rows of herringbone stitches.

4 With right sides together, pin one long edge of a heading flap along the top edge of a curtain piece, so that the edge of the heading is 1.5cm (⅝in) down from the top edge of the curtain. Stitch together, taking the seam allowance from the top edge of the heading. Turn the heading to the right side and press the seam flat, up towards the heading.

5 Fold under 1.5cm (⅝in) to the wrong side along the other long edge of the heading. Press and tack. Fold the heading in half lengthways so that the turned edge meets the sewing line on the back of the curtain. Slipstitch in place.

6 With the heading flat, pin heading tape on to the back of the curtain so that the bottom edge runs slightly below the heading stitching line. Cut the tape to fit, turning under the ends to neaten them. Machine stitch in place through all thicknesses of fabric.

strawberry ribbon throw

The throw pictured here has been cleverly used to cover up an old sofa, but it could be used to equal advantage over a bed, or even as a blanket in its own right. The border is cross stitched onto a pretty velvet ribbon which trims a soft, wool challis blanket. It is cross stitched here with a delicate strawberry pattern, but you can choose another design from a selection of alternatives which includes hearts, florals and cherries, which are featured on pages 106 and 107.

About the throw

Approximate finished size: 197 x 135cm (77½ x 53in)
Number of stitches per 2.5cm (1in): 14

You will need

7.25m (8yd) ribbon, at least 4cm (1½in) wide (We used cotton velvet for this throw. If you choose another type of ribbon make sure that it is firm)
2m (2¼ yd) fine woven wool fabric, 138cm (54in) wide (we used 100 per cent wool challis)
Waste canvas, 14 threads per 2.5cm (1in)
Crewel needle size 7 or 8
Stranded cotton in the colours specified below
Use two strands of thread throughout

To work the design

1 Following the threads, cut the waste canvas into strips. These should measure at least 4cm (1½in) wider each side than the ribbon.
2 Measure the ribbon carefully along the fabric, allowing approximately 5cm (2in) extra at the corners for the hem and overlap. Alternatively, if you prefer to mitre (see page 18), measure and cut the ribbon into four lengths.
3 Leaving approximately 5cm (2in) free for each corner, tack the waste canvas in place on to the first length of ribbon, checking that its threads are in line with the ribbon edges. You may find it easier to work with only a smallish piece of waste canvas each time.
4 Work the motifs from the chart, counting the threads on the canvas and allowing a space of three stitches between each motif. For mitred corners, leave an unstitched area of ribbon to turn under so that only whole motifs are visible.
5 Carefully remove the waste canvas one thread at a time.
6 Continue to work along the remaining lengths of ribbon in the same way.

To make up

1 Turn under the selvedges along both sides of the length of fabric and carefully hem in place. Carefully tack and lightly press the two remaining sides and then work a small double hem.
2 Pin, then tack the ribbon on to the right side of the fabric, overlapping or mitring the corners neatly.
3 Hand sew or machine stitch the ribbon in place along all four edges of the throw. Remove the tacking. Press lightly on the wrong side of the fabric, taking care not to flatten the stitching.

Thread colours

		Anchor	DMC
	crimson	19	347
	scarlet	46	666
	yellow	307	783
	dark green	268	3345
	green	266	3347
	ecru	372	738
	cream	885	3047
	rust	347	402
	brown	349	301
	green	845	3011
	chartreuse	907	832
	straw	956	677

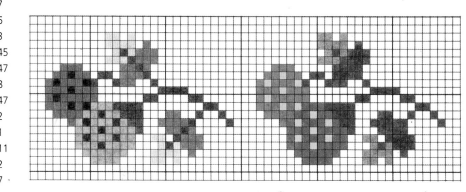

church sampler

Samplers play a significant part in the history of embroidery. Their stitched patterns have timeless charm, and the traditional motifs used to embellish them have particular character – the essence of birds, trees, houses and people are often captured in just a few carefully placed stitches.

Originally, samplers were used to provide a record of the different kinds of stitches and patterns for both professional and amateur needleworkers. Examples of these exist from the early sixteenth century. During the eighteenth and nineteenth centuries, they were more often used as a teaching exercise; most young girls were expected to work at least one sampler over the course of their education, usually including alphabets and numerals as part of the design. Towards the end of the nineteenth century samplers became appreciated much more for purely aesthetic reasons.

The next three projects involve samplers of quite different types, reflecting their development from the early days. By using the charts on pages 98–101 you can incorporate references to your own family in the samplers to make exquisite works of art both to decorate your home and to become treasured heirlooms.

About the sampler

Approximate finished size: 34 x 33cm
   (13½ x 13in), excluding frame
Number of stitches per 2.5cm (1in): 18
Work stitches over two threads at a time
   for the design, except the lettering,
   see below

You will need

73cm (29in) evenweave linen, 74cm
   (29½in) wide, 36 threads per 2.5cm
   (1in)
Tapestry needle size 26
Stranded cotton in the colours specified
   on pages 66–69
Use two strands of thread throughout

To work the design

1 Decide what lettering you would like to include. The stitches making the lettering on the original sampler were half the size of those of the rest of the sampler (although the letters can be up to eight stitches high, they are equal to the height of only four stitches of the rest of the design). To achieve this, work over one thread for the lettering, instead of two. Using the alphabets given on pages 98 –101, draft the lettering on to graph paper. What you choose is a matter of personal preference; you can either include references to your own family and home, or if you prefer, you can work a simple alphabet. Work out whether the lettering will look best over one or two lines. Bear in mind that each square on the chart is equal to two (half-size) lettering stitches.

2 Mark the position of the border on the fabric. Taking a side at a time, make one row of tacking stitches approximately 22cm (8½in) from one long edge, then make another row, running parallel to the first, but 17 stitches (34 threads) in from it.

3 Following the chart, stitch the outside border line (pale green) within the tacking lines until one corner is reached. Count and stitch the diagonal corner; then repeat the two tacking lines for the next side and stitch to the next corner. The dark green inside line of the border may be stitched either at this stage or later, whichever you prefer.

4 Once the border is completed, the other elements are easier to position. Begin with the church. Position its base by counting 40 stitches from the right border, 42 stitches from the left border and 3 stitches up from the lower border.

5 Next stitch the lettering (see step 1) in the space below the church. The flowers, trees and so on are now easier to place in relation to the border and church.

6 Trim the fabric, leaving a large enough border all around for mounting and framing the sampler (see page 19).

Thread colours

		Anchor	DMC				Anchor	DMC
	pink	1024	107			pale gold	887	422
	dark brown	358	433			ecru	390	3033
	light brown	375	420			flesh	880	951
	gold	373	3045			dark green	217	319

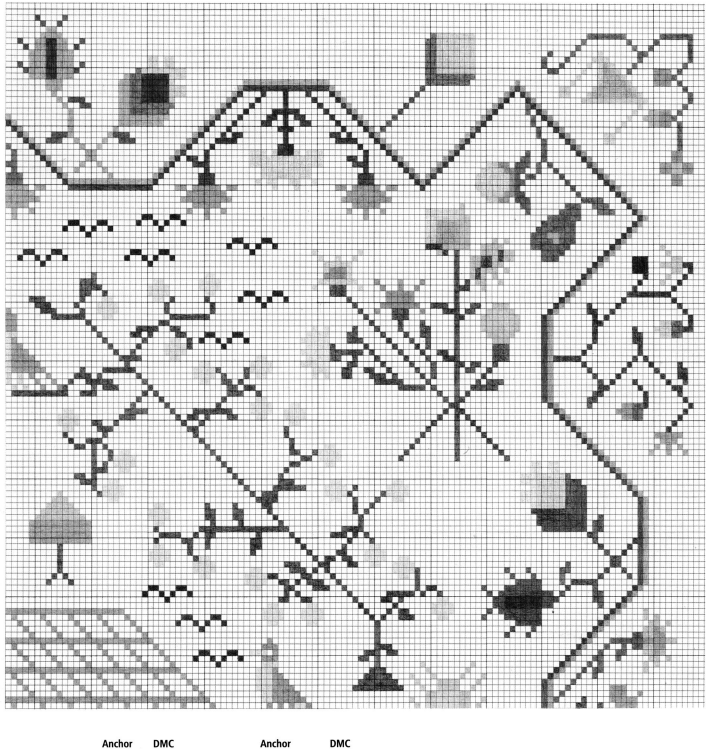

		Anchor	DMC			Anchor	DMC
	sage	860	3363		black	403	310
	leaf-green	843	3012				
	pale-green	854	3013				
	blue	168	807				

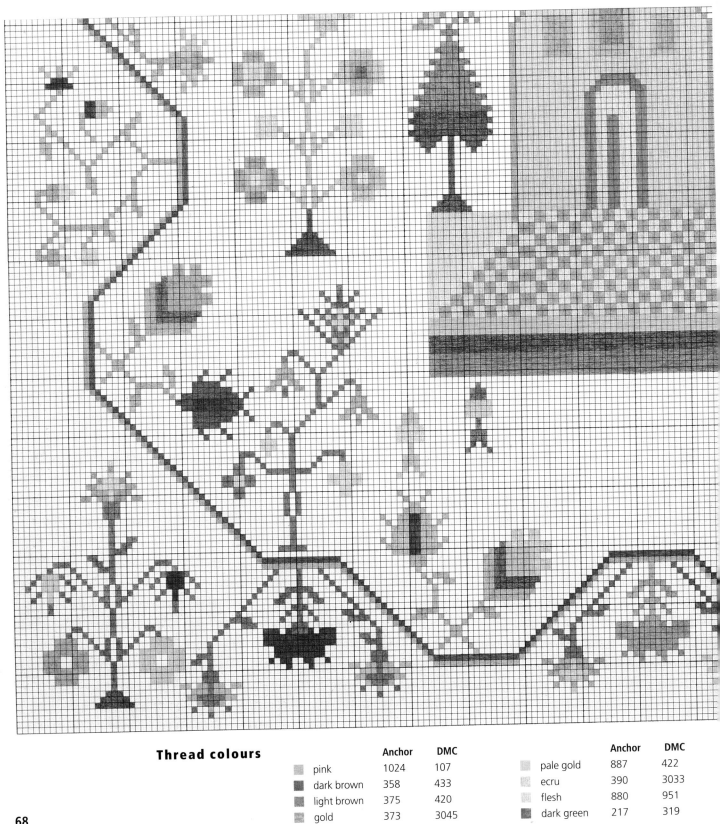

Thread colours

	Anchor	DMC			Anchor	DMC
pink	1024	107		pale gold	887	422
dark brown	358	433		ecru	390	3033
light brown	375	420		flesh	880	951
gold	373	3045		dark green	217	319

		Anchor	DMC			Anchor	DMC
▦	sage	860	3363	▦	black	403	310
▦	leaf-green	843	3012				
▧	pale-green	854	3013				
▦	blue	168	807				

school sampler

Old school samplers provide a wealth of inspiration for motifs and border designs, many of them looking just as fresh now as when they were originally worked. This Annan School sampler, stitched by Barbara Weall in 1870, features symmetrically arranged motifs of flowers and fruit baskets with a remarkably contemporary feel. Set out in three bold bands across the sampler, the urns and pots, filled with stylized blooms, capture the atmosphere of a formal garden. Initials of family members have been incorporated into the alphabet and a border of numerals has been stitched across the top.

It is easy to work your own family tree into a similar design, but if making this design seems over-ambitious, a scaled-down version, made up of a few pots of flowers contained within a border, would look just as special.

About the sampler

Approximate finished size: 63 x 49.5cm
   (24¾ x 19½in), excluding frame
Number of stitches per 2.5cm (1in): 14
Work stitches over two threads at a time
   when using fabric with double the
   thread count

You will need

89.5cm (35½in) evenweave linen,
   103cm (40¾in) wide, 28 threads per
   2.5cm (1in)
Tapestry needle size 24
Either stranded cotton, using two
   strands, or Paterna Persian wool, using
   one strand. The original piece was
   worked in wool on linen canvas, giving
   a textured, raised effect. In the charts
   on pages 72 –75, colours are given for
   stranded cotton, which will produce a
   less ridged, more refined result.

To work the design

1 Begin by deciding on the lettering to include in the sampler. Using the charted alphabet (see page 72), draft the letters on to graph paper and arrange them over one or two lines. Centre the lettering for ease of positioning (see step 5).

2 Start by stitching the inside line of the border in dark green. Mark 24cm (9½in) in from one short edge and work a straight horizontal line of 308 stitches along one long side, starting 24cm (9½in) in from the edge. This forms the base of the inside of the border.

3 Next work the short edges over 232

stitches, use the first and last stitches of the base row just worked as a guide for the bottom corners.

4 Work the top row in the same way. Counting down from the top row, work the three straight lines of the top lettering, then the three remaining horizontal lines running across the sampler.

5 Once these guidelines are in place it is up to you to decide which order you will work in.

It is helpful to tack a line down the centre of the fabric. This is useful as a guide to work the lettering, border, school and flower motifs.

6 Trim the fabric, leaving a large enough border all around for mounting and framing the sampler (see page 19).

Thread colours

		Anchor	DMC			Anchor	DMC
	red	47	304		sage	844	3012
	yellow	280	581		turquoise	779	926
	bottle	879	500		blue	921	931

		Anchor	DMC			Anchor	DMC
	grey	399	318		light brown	351	400
	black	403	310		beige	853	613
	brown	381	938		soft grey	388	3782

Thread colours

		Anchor	DMC			Anchor	DMC
	red	47	304		sage	844	3012
	yellow	280	581		turquoise	779	926
	bottle	879	500		blue	921	931

		Anchor	DMC			Anchor	DMC
	grey	399	318		light brown	351	400
	black	403	310		beige	853	613
	brown	381	938		soft grey	388	3782

sampler cushion

A sampler cushion is a practical way to show off your handiwork, at the same time adding a traditional element to a sitting room. Motifs of naturalistic subjects, such as animals, birds, trees and people, became especially popular during the nineteenth century when the purely decorative aspect of samplers began to be recognized. This sampler cushion design includes a menagerie of animals and a simple twining border embellished with flowers, orchard fruits and garden architecture. Incorporate motifs of family pets or favourite flowers to make it your own secret garden.

About the cushion

Approximate finished size: 45cm (18in) square

Number of stitches per 2.5cm (1in): 14

Work stitches over two threads at a time when using fabric with double the thread count

You will need

78 x 68cm (31 x 27in) Irish linen, 28 threads per 2.5cm (1in). The fabric should be tea-dyed (see page 19)

2 pieces matching fabric, 48cm (19¼in), for the cushion back

Cushion pad, 46cm (18 in) square, approximately

2m (2yd) piping or fringing (optional)

Tapestry needle size 24

Stranded cotton in the colours specified on page 78

Use two strands of thread throughout

The cushion photographed was made using Anchor threads, so to achieve an exact likeness you should use the same.

To work the design

1 Run two rows of tacking stitches – one lengthways, one widthways – through the centre of the fabric. Now run a line of tacking stitches 20cm (8in) in from the outer edge, all around the fabric, representing the size of the finished cushion.

2 Stitch the border outline working from the chart, beginning at the centre of one side and working eight stitches in from the tacking line.

3 Work the alphabet, starting at the centre and counting down from the border.

4 Work the ivy leaf pattern under the alphabet in the same way.

5 Once the border and the tacking lines are in place, you can use them as a guide when placing the other motifs, which you are free to stitch in any order.

To cut out

Before cutting or making any adjustments, check the measurements of the stitched piece carefully. Measuring an even border of plain fabric all around the stitched area, cut the embroidered piece to 48 x 32cm (19¼ x 12¾in); this includes a seam allowance on every side of 1.5cm (⅝in).

To make up

1 Fold under the 1.5cm (⅝in) seam allowance along the lower and upper edges of the embroidered piece and carefully press.

2 Pin the embroidery onto the right side of one piece of fabric, placing it centrally. Leave 9.5cm (3¾in) of the main fabric visible at the top and the bottom.

3 Using soft embroidery cotton, blanket stitch the embroidered piece to the main fabric along upper and lower edges.

4 If you decide to use piping or fringing, first tack it along the right side of the cushion piece, close to the sewing line. Make sure that the part of the fringe to be seen on the finished cushion lies to the inside of the seam line. Carefully ease or snip the trimming around corners.

5 With right sides together, tack, then machine stitch all around the cushion, leaving a gap large enough to insert the cushion pad. Carefully remove the tacking stitches.

6 Turn the cushion right side out and press the edges carefully, taking care not to flatten the piping or fringing if used.

7 Insert the cushion pad.

8 Close the opening with slipstitch.

Thread colours

		Anchor	DMC
	yellow	874	834
	gold	901	680
	sienna	375	420
	green	844	3012
	dark green	263	3362
	blue	977	334
	grey	847	3072
	pink	1027	3722
	rust	884	400
	brown	358	433
	dark brown	382	3371

Household items

This final section of cross stitch projects for the home includes a wealth of decorative ideas. Shelf edgings were once a common feature over the mantlepiece in both country cottages and town houses; in this chapter, teacup designs are used to enhance a shelf edging and a tea cosy.

Borders are always popular, and the one that is used here to decorate the huckaback towel could be exchanged for another of the designs illustrated on pages 106–107; in fact you could make a set of towels, stitching a different pattern along each border. The three linen bags show a different use for cross stitch. Appliqué motifs are attached to the bags with freehand cross stitches, that are also used to embellish the appliqué designs.

№ 106

shelf edging

This pretty teacup edging for a shelf or mantlepiece is easy to stitch once the motifs are positioned. Work them in one of the colour schemes shown on the charts here or on page 84; alternatively use your own scheme to match the decorations at home. This design would complement a collection of china which you want to show to its best advantage.

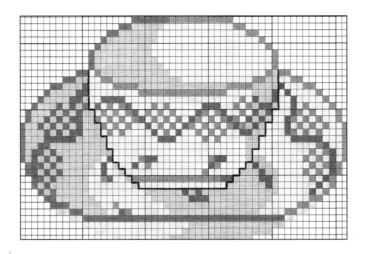

Thread colours

		Anchor	DMC
	cream	926	822
	grey	397	762
	china blue	978	322
	royal blue	979	312
	navy	922	930

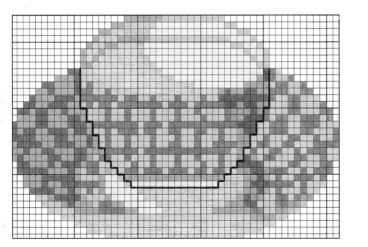

Thread colours

		Anchor	DMC
	cream	885	3047
	ecru	899	869
	yellow	307	783
	orange	337	922
	rust	339	920
	brown	341	918

About the shelf edging

Depth: 14cm (5½in)

Size of each motif: 12cm wide x 7cm high (4¾ x 2¾in)

Space between each motif: 3cm (1¼in) approximately

Number of stitches per 2.5cm (1in): 11

You will need

One piece natural Aida, 27cm (10⅝in) deep by required length, 11 threads per 2.5cm (1in). (Depth includes 11.5cm (4½in) to attach to top of shelf, adjustable if necessary)

Calico for lining, 15.5cm (6⅛in) deep by required length

Ribbon trim (optional), same length as the shelf

Tapestry needle size 24

Stranded cotton in the colours specified here and on page 84

Use two strands of thread throughout

To work the design

1 First work out the spacing of the motifs. In the sample shown here, the motifs are 52 stitches wide with a space of 14 stitches between them; therefore, each motif requires a total space of 66 stitches. Use these figures to calculate how many motifs will fit on your shelf edging: the size of the motif will remain constant (52 stitches), so adjust the space as necessary.

2 Run vertical tacking lines, approximately 14cm (5½in) long, from the lower edge of the fabric. Position them at 66-stitch intervals (adjust for your spacing) to indicate the centre of each motif.

3 Position the bottom row of motifs 4.5cm (1¾in) up from lower edge of the fabric, matching the centre of the chart to the tacking lines.

4 Stitch the motifs following the charts.

5 Remove the tacking stitches.

To make up

1 With right sides together and taking a 1.5cm (⅝in) seam allowance, tack, then sew the calico lining to the bottom edge of the stitched fabric. Turn to the right side and press the double thickness.

2 Pin the ribbon trim to the shelf edging, through all the layers, 13cm (5in) up from the lower edge, so that it runs along the shelf edge.

3 Tack and stitch the ribbon and lining. Remove the tacking.

4 Attach the edging to the shelf top with the spare fabric, using tacks or glue.

tea cosy

Worked in the same attractive design as the shelf edging, this tea cosy has a thick lining for good insulation which will help to keep your tea piping hot! Stitch the tea cosy using the chart below or alternatively choose the same colour scheme as the shelf edging, the two make a charming, complementary pair; and the tea cosy will happily grace any kitchen table for many years to come.

About the tea cosy

Approximate finished size: 39cm wide x
  26cm high (15¼ x 10¼in)
Size of each motif: 12 x 7.5cm (4⅝ x 3in)
Space between each motif: 3cm (1½in)
Number of stitches per 2.5cm (1in): 11

You will need

42 x 15.5cm (16½ x 6¼in) natural Aida,
  11 stitches per 2.5cm (1in)
30cm (18in) cotton fabric 110cm (43in)
  wide (we used cotton herringbone
  in ecru)
60cm (24 in) cotton lining fabric 110cm
  (43in) wide
2 pieces wadding, 42 x 29cm (16½ x
  11½in)
Tissue paper
Tapestry needle size 24
Stranded cotton in the colours specified
  left.
Use two strands of thread throughout

To work the design

1 Run two vertical lines of tacking stitches about 13cm (5in) in from the two short edges of the Aida, indicating the centres of the two motifs.

2 Placing the bottom row of motifs 4cm (1½in) up from the lower edge of the fabric, match the centre of the chart to the tacking lines and stitch the motifs, working from the chart.
3 Remove the tacking stitches.

To make up

1 Make a tissue paper template of the tea cosy. Begin with a rectangle measuring 42 x 29cm (16½ x 11½in). Draw, then cut out, a curve on one side. Fold the tissue paper in half and cut the other side to match.
2 Cut out two pieces of both the cotton fabric and the wadding. Cut out four pieces of lining fabric in the same way .
3 Measure and fold under a 1.5cm (⅝in) seam along the upper edge of the embroidered trim. Press the seam flat.
4 With right sides facing, lay the embroidered trim over one piece of fabric so that the bottom edges line up. Tack, then slipstitch the upper edge of the trim to the fabric.
5 With right sides together, tack, then sew a 1.5cm (⅝in) seam around the curved edge of the fabric pieces. Do the same with both pairs of lining pieces, but take a seam allowance of 2cm (¾in). Do not stitch the lower edge of either of the linings. Snip the curves where necessary, press and remove the tacking.
6 Turn one of the linings right side out and put the second one inside it. Push the two pieces of wadding in between. Turn in the bottom edges of both linings and hand sew together. Make a few random quilting stitches right through the lining and wadding to hold it in place.
7 Fold under and press a turning of 1.5cm (⅝in) along the lower edges of the cosy cover. Insert the inner piece and slipstitch to the cover along the lower edge.

Thread colours

	Anchor	DMC
cream	885	3047
dark cream	880	951
yellow	891	676
gold	313	977
pale pink	75	3354
dark pink	77	3350
pale green	876	503
dark green	878	501

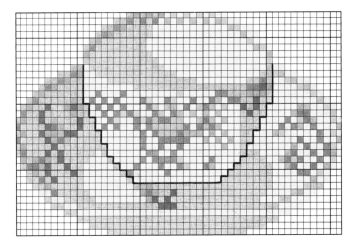

huckaback towel

Linen is robust, hardwearing and highly absorbent, making it an ideal fabric for hand and bath towels. Huck weave linen is traditionally used for this purpose and has a classic elegance that is hard to match.

Old huckaback towels can be found in junk shops, often in good condition, which testifies to the enduring qualities of linen. Embellish them with geometric, floral or leafy borders chosen from the charts on pages 106–107. The regular 'pip' marks, which form the texture of this fabric, are simple to use as a guide for plotting cross stitch patterns.

About the towel

Approximate finished size: 61 x 112cm
   (24 x 44in)
Number of stitches per 2.5cm (1in): 13

You will need

88cm (35in) huckaback linen, 61cm
   (24in) wide
or an old huckaback towel
1.3m (1½yd) lace or openwork edging,
   13cm (5in) deep
Crewel needle size 6 or 7
Stranded cotton in the colours below
Use two strands of thread throughout

To work the design

Depending on the weave of the fabric, the number of threads per 2.5cm (1in) may vary, thus altering the scale of the border, so before beginning it will be necessary to calculate how many stitches should be worked to the centimetre/inch.
1 Fold the linen in half lengthways and mark the centre fold with a line of tacking stitches, following the grain of the fabric indicated by the pips in the textured weave.
2 Measure 2.5cm (1in) in from the short edge of the fabric and use pins to mark a line the length of the short edge, then make a row of tacking stitches, following the grain of the fabric. This line marks the bottom edge of the border.
3 Stitch the border, plotting the design from the centre of the chart and the tacked central line on the cloth, working out towards the long edges.
4 Work the other end of the cloth in the same way if required.
5 Remove the tacking stitches.

To make up

1 Along both short ends of the fabric, turn under 5mm (¼in) twice to the wrong side. Slipstitch in place. If possible leave the long edges as selvedges, but if the fabric has been cut to size, it will be necessary to turn small double hems in the same way.
2 Cut a length of openwork or lace edging to fit both short ends of the hemmed fabric. Neaten the side edges with tiny hems. Press lightly.
3 Pin and tack the edging to the fabric and slipstitch neatly in place. Press to complete.

Thread colours

		Anchor	DMC
■	blue	848	927
▨	pink	838	3064

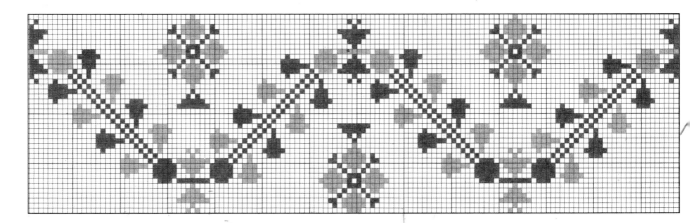

three linen bags

Unusual bags made from scraps of colourful fabric provide useful and attractive storage places for keeping gym or ballet shoes tidy or for hiding used clothing while it awaits wash day. Ticking stripes and check fabrics, mixed together for the appliqué patches, give these laundry bags a folk art appeal. Freehand cross stitches fix the patches in place and any uneven stitching adds to their charm, making these perfect projects for anyone whose stitching lacks precision. Tiny pearl and linen buttons can be used for extra decoration, picking up the detail of the garments depicted in the motifs. If the ticking colours look too new, try using the wrong side of the fabric; it often has a more faded appearance which is especially appealing for this style of project.

42cm (12¼ x 16½in).

2 For the draw cord channel, cut two strips of contrasting fabric, each 31 x 10cm (12¼ x 3¼in).

To make up

1 With right sides facing, pin and tack the back and front together along the sides and the bottom edges. Stitch, then turn to the right side and press.

2 With right sides facing, stitch the draw cord channel strips together along a short edge and press the seam flat. Turn under 1.5cm (⅝in) to the wrong side on both remaining short edges and stitch in place. Turn the same amount along both long edges, press and tack.

3 Fold the strip in half lengthways. Place the folded strip over the raw edges of the top of the bag to encase it, ensuring that the open ends of the strip meet at a side seam. Tack, then work a row of cross stitches along the edge of the strip on the outside of the bag. Slipstitch the strip to the inside of the bag and join the ends.

4 Thread the ribbon through the channel to make a loop and pin the ends. Cut two matching triangles from a scrap of fabric. Turn in the edges and slipstitch together, feed the ends of the ribbon into the triangle before stitching up the third side.

Shoe bag

About the bag

Approximate finished size of bag:
  29 x 41cm (11½ x 18½in)
Seam allowances are 1.5cm (⅝in)

You will need

50cm (½yd) ticking fabric x 142cm (56in)
10cm (¼yd) contrasting fabric, 90cm
  (36in) wide, for draw cord channel
1.2m (1¼yd) grosgrain ribbon, 17mm
  (¾in) wide, for draw cord
Assorted fabric oddments
Tracing paper
Crewel needle size 6 or 7
Pearl cotton thread in assorted colours

To cut out

1 For the front and back of the bag, cut two rectangles of ticking, each 31 x

To work the design

1 Trace the shoe motifs from the outlines below to make pattern pieces, then cut the two shoes from a contrasting fabric. Cut two pieces from another fabric to make the shapes for inside the shoes. Turn under 5mm (¼in) around all the pieces, snipping curves where necessary. Tack around the edges, then press.

2 Pin, then tack the shoe shapes to the bag, then position the shapes for inside the shoes and tack them in place. Work evenly spaced cross stitches around the edges of the shapes to fix them in place.

3 Use tiny cross stitches to hold down lengths of thread, representing the flaps for the laces and the place where the shoe upper meets the sole. Add more cross stitches at random to decorate the shoes to your own taste.

4 Using two strands of thread, stitch through the fabric to make long loops similar to shoe laces. Tie them in a bow, finishing off the ends with small knots. Work freehand cross stitches in a random arrangement around the shoes, or you can follow the illustration if you prefer.

5 Remove tacking to complete.

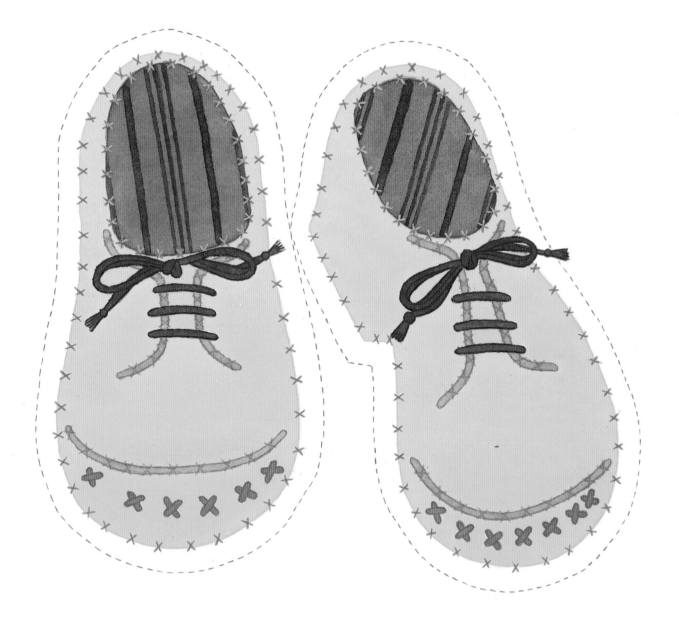

Lingerie bag

About the bag

Approximate finished size of bag:
  36 x 54cm (14 x 21in)
Seam allowances are 1.5cm (⅝in)

You will need

60cm (¾yd) ticking fabric x 142cm (56in)
10cm (¼yd) contrasting fabric, 90cm
  (36in) wide, for draw cord channel
90cm (1yd) ribbon, 2.5cm (1in) wide
2.5m (2½yd) grosgrain ribbon, 17mm
  (¾in) wide, for draw cord
Assorted fabric oddments
Small buttons
Tracing paper
Crewel needle size 6 or 7
Pearl cotton thread in assorted colours

To cut out

1 For the front and back of the bag, cut two rectangles of ticking, each 54.5 x 40cm (21½ x 15¾in).
2 For the draw cord channel, cut two strips of contrasting fabric, each 7 x 39cm (2¾ x 15½in).
3 For the tabs at the ends of the draw cord, cut two pieces of fabric, each 15 x 9cm (5¾ x 3½in).

To make up

1 Turn 1.5cm (⅝in) to the wrong side along both long edges of each draw cord channel strip. Turn under 1.5cm (⅝in) to the wrong side along the short edges of both strips. Slipstitch in place.
2 Place a channel strip on to the front fabric piece, parallel with a short edge (this will be the top of the bag) and 9cm (3½in) below the edge. Position it centrally so that it is within the side seam allowance of the main fabric. Tack then work rows of cross stitches along both edges to secure. Join the second channel strip to the back piece in the same way.
3 With right sides together, pin the front and back, and stitch along the side and base edges. Turn to right side and press.
4 Fold the edging ribbon in half lengthways and press. Push the folded ribbon over the raw edge along the top of the bag, trimming away any excess ribbon where the ends meet. Tack, then work cross stitches through all thicknesses of fabric along the ribbon edge.
5 Halve the grosgrain ribbon and thread through the channel from each side opening, to make two draw cord loops that pull from each side.
6 Make tabs to complete the ends of the draw cords. With right sides facing, fold the piece of fabric in half, bringing the short ends together. Stitch and turn right side out and press the seam allowance to the inside along the open edge. Push the ends of the draw cord inside the tab and stitch down. Make the second tab in the same way. Remove tacking.

To work the design

Make patches with appliqué motifs following the instructions for the laundry duffel bag (page 95), decorating the slip, bra and pants motifs with cross stitches and small linen or pearl buttons.

Laundry duffel bag

About the bag

Approximate finished size of bag:
69cm high x 90cm in diameter (27 x 35½in)
Seam allowances are 1.5cm (⅝in)

You will need

1.1m (1¼yd) ticking fabric x 142cm (56in)
20cm (¼yd) calico, 90cm (36in) wide
Assorted fabric oddments
Small buttons
Tracing paper
Crewel needle size 6 or 7
Pearl cotton thread in assorted colours

To cut out

1 Cut a rectangle of ticking, 120 x 68cm (47¼ x 26¾in), for the main piece.
2 Cut a circle of ticking, 39cm (15¼in) in diameter, for the base.
3 For the draw cord, cut two strips of calico, each 8 x 76cm (3¼ x 30in).
4 For the draw cord tabs, cut 14 rectangles from the fabric oddments as follows: two pieces 23 x 15cm (9 x 6in), five pieces 13 x 15cm (5 x 6in), seven pieces 16 x 15cm (6¼ x 6in).
5 Cut a piece of fabric 9 x 15cm (3½ x 6in), to make the tab at the end of the draw cord.

To make up

1 Fold the main piece in half, right sides facing, bringing the side edges together. Pin and stitch to make a tube.
2 Machine stitch a line all around the base circle, 1.2cm (½in) in from the edge. Snip up to the stitching line at regular intervals all around the circle.
3 With right sides together, pin and tack the base circle into the bottom end of the tube. Stitch and clip the seams to fit.
4 Make a hem along the top edge of the bag, taking a turning of 1cm (⅜in), followed by a second turning of 1.5cm (⅝in). Tack and stitch close to the edge of the hem.
5 Make the draw cord tabs as follows: with right sides facing, fold a fabric piece in half lengthways. Stitch down the long edge to make a tube, then turn to the right side. Turn the seam allowance to the inside of the tube along both raw ends. Tack and press flat. Machine stitch all around the tab, close to the edge. Make all 14 tabs in the same way.
6 Fold each tab in half and pin it along the top edge of the bag to make fixed loops, each projecting 3.5cm (1½in) above the edge. Space them evenly, with the different lengths randomly placed. On the outside of the bag, attach the tabs with freehand cross stitches along their edges; on the inside, slipstitch them in place.
7 To make the draw cord, sew the two strips of calico together along one short edge, right sides together. Press the seam

allowance to the wrong side along both long edges of the strip. Fold in half lengthways, wrong sides facing, so that these turned edges meet. Stitch all along the strip, close to the edge and through all thicknesses.

8 Thread the draw cord through the tabs along the top of the bag. Pin, then stitch the ends together.

9 Make the end tab in the following way. With right sides facing, fold the piece of fabric in half bringing the short edges together. Stitch along two sides. Turn to the right side and press the seam allowance to the inside along the open edge. Push the ends of the draw cord inside the tab and stitch close to the edge to secure.

To work the design

1 Trace the glove shape on to paper to make a pattern piece and use this to cut out a glove from a scrap of fabric. Turn under 5mm (¼in) to the wrong side all around the piece, snipping curves where necessary. Tack all around the edge. Work a row of tiny cross stitches on the glove for cuff detail and decorate with three tiny buttons.

2 Cut a 15cm (6in) square from a contrasting fabric scrap, turn under 1cm (⅜in) all around, tack and press. Place the glove diagonally on the fabric square and tack in place. Work evenly spaced cross stitches all around the glove shape to join the pieces together, as well as to decorate the patch.

3 Make the other patch motifs (see overleaf) in the same way. Cut them out of fabric scraps and add buttons and cross stitches to decorate. Cut rectangles of contrasting fabric to back each shape. Cut enough fabric to leave a border all around the shape, remembering to allow for 1cm (⅜in) turnings on each edge.

4 Cut a few smaller patches to arrange among the larger ones and turn under the edges in the same way as before. Arrange the patches at random on the bag as required, pinning, then tacking them in position. Stitch the patches in place with cross stitches worked along the edges.

5 Remove the tacking stitches.

Patterns & motifs

In this chapter you will find a host of extra motifs to use, both as an alternative to some of the designs found in the earlier chapters and also for your own projects. There is a choice of different alphabets that can be used with monograms and samplers; a wealth of delightful miniature motifs from animals and flowers to hearts, keys, and crowns; and finally a selection of borders, medallions, and corner motifs.

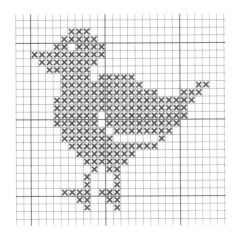

alphabets &
numerals

See Samplers on pages 64–79

Here and on the following pages you will find three alternative alphabets to use when working the samplers and the cushion featured in the chapter: In the sitting room. The numerals can be worked on to the Napkin Rings (see page 51), and you can use the larger numbers to decorate the Cot Blanket. The alphabets and numerals can be transferred on to either a larger, or a smaller grid. This will increase or reduce the size of the finished motifs, enabling you to create an alphabet to the size of your choice, to complement your own design.

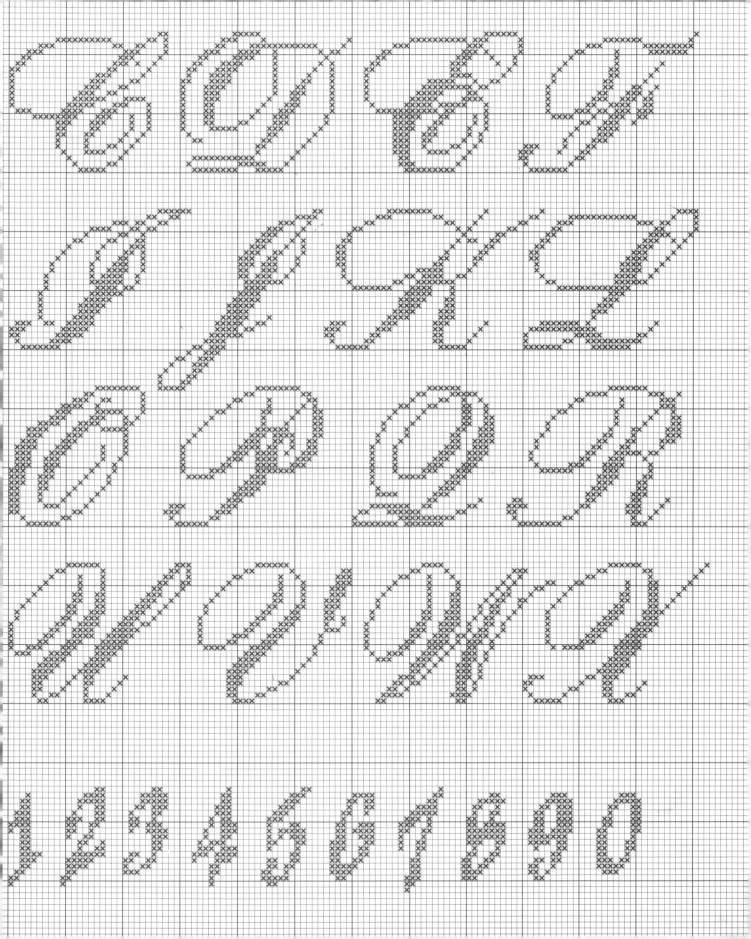

flowers, trees & mini-motifs

See Samplers on pages 64–79

Choose from this selection of elaborate floral and tree motifs when stitching the samplers and Sampler Cushion, (see pages 64–79). The range of mini-motifs on the two following pages offer a choice of animals, fruit, and flowers, around which you can design a unique sampler of your own. For a regal feel, we have also included some hearts, crowns, and keys, which would be suitable for either the Monogrammed Pillowcase (see page 34), or the Napkin Rings (see page 51).

traditional borders

See Huckaback Towel on page 86

**The borders shown on these two pages
give you a choice of designs for the
curtain panel border (see page 60), the
Ribbon Throw (see page 62), or the
Huckaback Towel (see page 86). Be sure
to work the borders from the centre
outwards to ensure a full pattern repeat.**

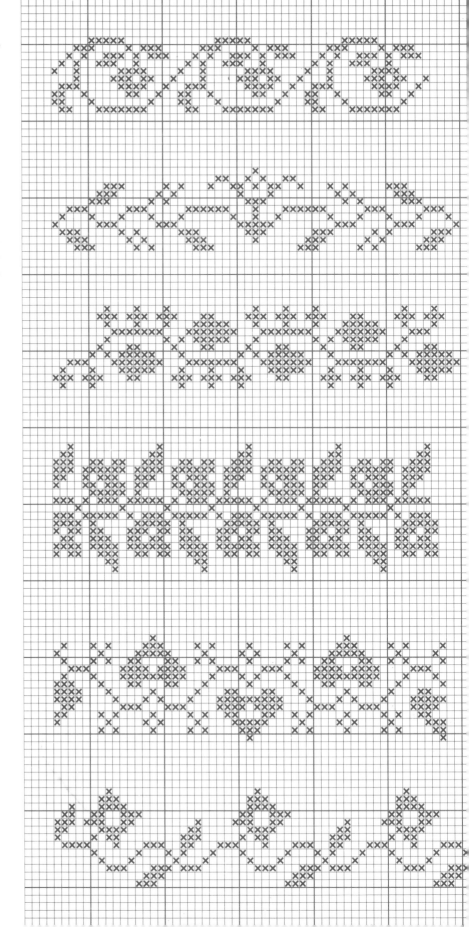

106

medallions & corner motifs

See Gingham Tablemats on pages 48–49

These traditional 'snowflake' medallion motifs, and decorative corners can be effectively used as an alternative to the one on the Gingham Tablemats (see pages 48 and 49). You could also use them on a project of your own choice by placing the medallions in straight lines, as borders, or in an all-over pattern.

108

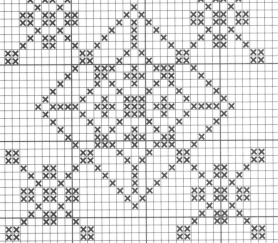
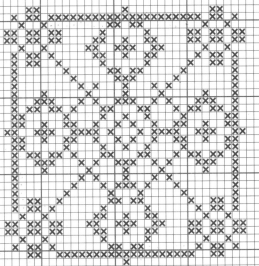

index

acknowledgements

The author would like to thank the following people for their considerable contributions which have made this book possible: Shirley Bradford for using her exceptional technical expertise to interpret some of the antique designs and for charting and originating many of the patterns; Alice Nicol for making many of the projects and samples for photography with great enthusiasm at a moment's notice and with such care and precision and also for her continuing support; Vicky Brooks for designing and making the linen bags; Sarah Clarke for making up projects; Coats Crafts UK, in particular Stephanie Baker in the design department, for technical assistance and contributing the sampler cushion and teacup projects; DMC for supplying fabrics for photography; The Minton Archives for permission to use their designs as inspiration for the shelf edging and teacosy projects; Deborah Schneebeli-Morell for the crown and heart designs for the chair covers; Karen Spurgin for stitching the designs on the chair covers; and The Irish Linen Guild.

For the loan of pieces of cross stitch from their collections: Katrin Cargill, Mary Musto, Deborah Schneebeli-Morrell, Marilyn Garrow, Rebecca Scott Jarrett at Witney Antiques for helping to source the samplers and organising the loan of the church sampler, Kate Shin at Decorative Textiles and Lesley Hackett at Annan & Eskdale District Council for the loan of the school sampler. This sampler is reproduced by permission of Annandale and Eskdale District Council.

For supplying materials for the projects: The Blue Door, Streets, Sanderson, V V Rouleaux, Ian Mankin.